CONFRONTATION AT LEPANTO

CONFRONTATION AT LEPANTO

Christendom vs. Islam

T. C. F. HOPKINS

A TOM DOHERTY ASSOCIATES BOOK ★ NEW YORK

Edited by Pat LoBrutto

Maps © 2006 Chelsea Quinn Yarbro

A Forge Book
Published by Tom Doherty Associates, LLC
175 Fifth Avenue
New York, NY 10010

www.tor.com

Forge® is a registered trademark of Tom Doherty Associates, LLC.

Library of Congress Cataloging-in-Publication Data

Hopkins, T. C. F.
Confrontation at Lepanto : Christendom vs. Islam / T. C. F. Hopkins.—1st ed.
p. cm.
ISBN 0-765-30538-0
EAN 978-0-765-30538-1
1. Lepanto, Battle of, Greece, 1571—Fiction. I. Title.
DR516.H67 2006
956.93´01—dc22
2005032929

First Edition: July 2006

Printed in the United States of America

0 9 8 7 6 5 4 3 2 1

For
JACK THE FROG
for encouragement when it counted

T HE AUTHOR WOULD like to thank Milton Davis, Kamal Norjat, Jenny Sauers, and E. E. White for their review of this manuscript, and the corrections and suggestions they offered for its improvement. Also, thanks to fellow-Berkelean Chelsea Quinn Yarbro for preparing the maps included in the material of this work.

CONTENTS

Map of the Mediterranean Basin 10
Map of the Gulf of Patmas 12

Preface 13

1. The Eve of Battle 19
2. The Ottoman Empire 29
3. The Venetians 39
4. The Hapsburgs 49
5. Meanwhile, in the Rest of the World 55
6. Getting Personal 59
7. Opening Gambits 75
8. First Lull 81
9. Famagusta 87
10. A Change in Fortune 93
11. Reneging 97
12. European Preparation 103
13. Complications 111
14. Ottoman Preparation 115
15. Finding the Foe 119
16. The Point of No Return 125
17. Opening Moves 131
18. Uchiali 137
19. Interludes 143
20. Battle's End 145
21. First Reckoning 149
22. Developments 157
23. Reactions Spread 163
24. In Constantinople 167
25. More Repercussions 173
26. Don Juan de Austria 181
27. Venetian Dénouement 187
28. Don Juan's Dénouement 191
29. Afterthoughts 197

Index 199

ATLANTIC OCEAN

ENGLAND

NETHERLANDS

SPANISH HAPSBURG TERRITORY

FRANCE

AUST

Venice

VENETIAN EMPIRE

ADRIATIC SEA

Genoa

PAPAL STATES

CORSICA

SPANISH HAPSBURG TERRITORY

BALEARIC ISLANDS

SARDINIA

Messin

SICILY

SPANISH PORTS

Tunis

MALTA

MEDITERRANEAN S

THE MEDITERRANEAN BASIN,
EUROPE, AND THE NEAR EAST
1571

OTTOMAN TERRITORY

European borders —— ·· — ·· —

Ottoman borders ∶ ∶ ∶ ∶ ∶ ∶ ∶

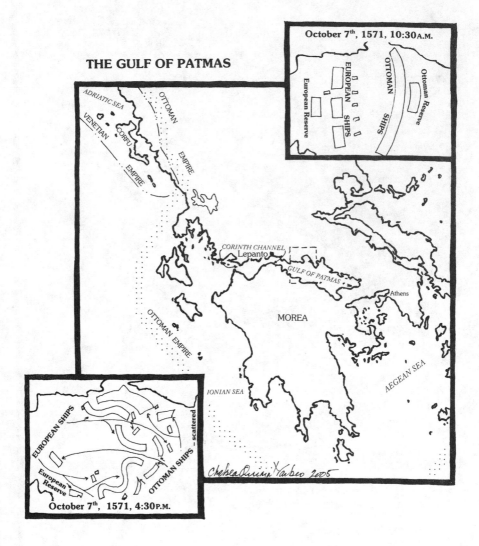

THE GULF OF PATMAS

October 7th, 1571, 10:30 A.M.

EUROPEAN SHIPS

European Reserve

OTTOMAN SHIPS

Ottoman Reserve

ADRIATIC SEA

VENETIAN EMPIRE

CORFU

OTTOMAN EMPIRE

CORINTH CHANNEL
Lepanto

GULF OF PATMAS

MOREA

Athens

OTTOMAN EMPIRE

IONIAN SEA

AEGEAN SEA

EUROPEAN SHIPS

European Reserve

OTTOMAN SHIPS – scattered

October 7th, 1571, 4:30 P.M.

ChelseaQuinn Yarbro 2005

PREFACE

HISTORY OFTEN NEGLECTS naval battles, except when they are sufficiently significant or recent enough to be within living memory, in large part because naval battles rarely leave much in the way of aftermath, except for the survivors: unlike land battles, naval conflicts end without the kind of lasting destruction seen when a city is conquered, or a region is annexed by an invader. There is no scorched earth, no razed walls, no dramatic shifts in population. Such encounters as land campaigns provide usually result in ongoing hardships for the defeated, and occasionally the victors as well; there are often monuments—glorious or ironic—of the battles that provide a constant reminder of those past events. The environment recovers slowly from land battles, but not so for those fought on water.

In the case of naval battles most of the evidence lies under the waves, neither side of the dispute readily distinguished one from the other where they fall, and aside from occasional bits that wash up from time to time and the later discoveries of salvage operators and marine archeologists, long-term effects are absent. The sea itself is almost never permanently altered due to naval battles; in fact, when battles occur beyond the sight of land, the impact of such engagements tends to be military or diplomatic instead of societal—even the economic impact is diffuse—and not as intensely present in the public awareness as land conflicts. Add to that inaccessibility the disproportionate loss of life in naval battles due not to the fighting itself, but to the basic hazard of travel to all those who go down to the sea in ships—drowning—and it is easy to see how the general understanding of such battles is often as much imagination as fact, and as much rumor as reportage.

Since all battles are by nature hectic and confusing—whether on

land or sea, or in the air for that matter—keeping track of what is taking place is difficult for observers and participants alike. This is especially true for naval battles, not only because so much is going on, but
because in naval battles, particularly those before the twentieth century, smoke from cannon, flaming arrows, and burning ships tended
to obscure already bewildering events. Even in these days of instanta-
neous communications, satellite monitoring, torpedoes that report
on their positions right up to the instant of impact, and radar and
sonar to mark actual positions, naval battles are often more baffling
than land ones, and reports are faulty as a result, not from any intention to mislead, but because of the nature of the encounters.

At the time of Lepanto the quality of reportage was not as accurate
as the standards of the present day impose; the few surviving accounts available, as noted above, tend to be inherently contradictory,
not simply out of any desire to distort the actuality to accommodate a
religious, military, or political agenda, but because the actuality could
not be accurately observed by anyone, a problem hardly limited to
this one engagement, but making concision all but impossible for the
specific actions and times of the action. Add to the official records remaining the expectation and demands of politics and religion—
which is why they have survived—and it is astonishing that there is
any cohesion in what records we have to work from. There are also a
few fragmental reports, such as the brief account by a Thomas Hogg
or Hodge, hanged for piracy in Bermuda in 1582, who claimed to have
fought with the Dutch at Lepanto, and described the condition of the
Ottoman ships at the end of the engagement in his appeal to the
court for clemency. It is from such accounts that history must approach the battle; the reports and the outcome are the only present
means we have to determine the significance of Lepanto—or any
other battle, for that matter.

More than many of the clashes between Europeans and Ottomans,
Lepanto clearly delineates the cultural differences at work on both

sides of the conflict, and the various levels of misunderstandings that prevailed at the time, many of which continue to this day. Both Ottoman and European cultures then—as now—were ethnically diverse but more or less united by religion. This inclined each side to see the other as homogeneous rather than diverse, and that, in turn, created significant errors in assessments that inclined both sides to act upon assumptions of uniformity that did not exist. In considering Lepanto, there is an opportunity to adjust current-day perceptions to a more culturally comprehensive parallax, for as many dissimilarities as 1571 has to the present, it has many commonalities, as well.

In considering the various accounts of Lepanto, it may be useful to keep in mind that in the millennia before reliable communications were part of warfare, naval battles were often viewed as more defined by the realms of speculation than by any precise, disinterested historical record, and occasional accounts of survivors were inclined over time to improve in the telling. Few sailors were literate, and those who were usually decided to make the most of their talents and shaped their memories to suit their audience.

While unofficial contemporary accounts of Lepanto exist, such as the Hogg/Hodge one, there are gaps and unidentifiable divergences in the records of it, for although the battle was fought within sight of land, reliable witnesses are relatively few in spite of—or because of—the fact that it was reported fairly quickly after it took place, and to a highly interested public. The effects wrought as a result of the battle changed the balance of power at the time, yet it did not have the same reality as the land campaigns of the Ottoman Empire, and is often overlooked as the crucial turning point it is in the ongoing conflict between the Middle East and Europe—a conflict, as has been noted, that has not yet completely been resolved.

T. C. F. HOPKINS

CONFRONTATION AT LEPANTO

1

THE EVE OF BATTLE

O N THE COOL, blustery first Sunday in October, 1571, in what would come to be called the Gulf of Lepanto in Greece, a crucial naval battle took place between the formidable Ottoman Empire, centered in Constantinople and controlling most of the eastern and southern Mediterranean, as well as the trade routes associated with that vast region, and the cobbled-together Holy League of western European powers, controlling the northern and western Mediterranean Basin. At issue was the matter of control of the seas, and by extension, all seagoing trade which was the commercial lifeblood of port cities from the farthest end of the Black Sea to the Atlantic Ocean, and the economies of more than a dozen countries caught up in the dispute. It was the second time they had fought there in seventy-two years.

This battle was the culmination of more than three centuries of growing maritime military tensions, one of a long series of skirmishes and engagements fought primarily on the Mediterranean, Adriatic, Ionian, Aegean, and Black Seas, and the Sea of Marmora, just as Ottoman expansion kept pace on land, conquering much of Greece, Bulgaria, Bosnia, Serbia, Hungary, and lower Romania by the sixteenth century. This united effort, successful for over a century, was finally put to an end at Lepanto. The European ships were outnumbered and by count of weapons, out-cannoned by the Ottoman naval forces, but numbers do not tell the whole story.

The naval targets of choice that led to this battle—for the Ottoman forces—were primarily not military, but the so-called round ships of European merchants, which tended to be heavily laden, and therefore slower and less maneuverable than the European warships; their cargoes made them worth raiding, and as the easy pickings they were, the Ottoman Empire had pursued since the time of the Crusades. The goods they carried and the crews enriched both the captains of the ships and the Ottoman Empire, giving the Turks little motive to cease their predation. The European motives were somewhat more complicated, associated as they were with the growing religious strife coupled with a volatile political situation in Europe, which made alliances, even against a common foe, tricky.

Since scoring a major naval victory against the powerful Venetians in 1499, the Ottoman Turks had become increasingly brazen in their attacks on all European vessels, seizing cargo for plunder and hapless crews and passengers as slaves, behavior that grew bolder and more ruthless with passing time, so that by 1550, the European merchants had to modify their round ships to a more military design—not as broad in the beam, and with reinforced decks to accommodate more cannon; they began to send their merchant ships out in large flotillas with armed fighting war galleys to protect them, which brought about a more concerted attack-strategy among the Ottoman naval forces, for although the risks were greater with the war-galley escorts, the rewards were commensurately rich.

Ottoman expansion spread the maritime war until it reached from Gibraltar to the eastern end of the Black Sea. The situation on land was not any less fractious: by 1500, the Ottoman Empire was attempting to make permanent inroads into the Carpathian and Balkan Mountains and turning toward the major cities of eastern Europe with the clear intention of conquering as much territory as it could. There had been incursions into southern Spain and France, as well, made possible by the Ottoman presence in the Mediterranean, and the Europeans feared—with good cause—that there was more and worse to come, especially since, unlike the fairly unified Turks, the Europeans were unable to find sufficient common cause to make a concerted cooperative attempt to stop the land advancements of the Ottoman armies.

The maritime combatants had been at odds over more than territory: the European forces, optimistically but inaccurately called the Holy League, were made up of an uneasy, loose federation of soldiers, sailors, and leaders of the Austrian Hapsburg holdings, Spanish-Netherlands Hapsburg possessions, the Empire of the Most Serene Republic of Venice, the Republic of Genoa (firmly under Spanish control), the Papal States in central Italy, the Two Sicilies (which belonged to Spain), and Christian volunteers from as far away as Scotland and Scandinavia, all of whom saw the Ottoman Empire as a threat to Christendom as well as to the economy of Europe, and sufficiently menacing to require fairly united opposition.

The Ottoman Empire, which had cemented its dominance of what had been the Byzantine Empire when it occupied the Greek Christian stronghold and capital of Constantinople in 1453, was Turkish, controlling a vast conglomeration of Turks, Arabs, Berbers, Persians, Kurds, Syrians, Egyptians, Huns, Mongols, Armenians, Greeks, Bosnians, Serbs, Romanians, Albanians, Macedonians, Bulgars, and many other minor groups; most were Islamic, but not all, for pockets of Christian Orthodoxy remained in Ottoman territory, left over from the Byzantine Empire, which the Ottoman Empire supplanted. There were also Coptic Christians in Egypt and Ethiopia whose faith went largely unchallenged so long as the Copts made no active resistance to the Ottoman presence.

Islamic tradition demanded respect for "People of The Book," meaning those worshipping the God of Abraham, and so, officially at least, conversion to Islam was not required for Christians and Jews living within the bounds of the Ottoman Empire, although very few unconverted Christians were allowed to advance beyond the most minor bureaucratic posts unless they were eunuchs, and Jews were rarely granted positions of power, although many of the Sultans actively sought out Jewish advisors in a kind of traditional tokenism, to show allegiance to Abraham and to maintain the appearance of piety for The Book. In spite of tradition and the desire for continuity, such advancement was available only to a very, very few Jews, and those were generally wealthy men with good commercial connections.

In addition to the restrictive policies already noted, many Christian communities had to pay double taxes, occupy specially designated parts of towns and cities, and submit their sons to military draft for the privilege of keeping their faith; such burdens were not usually placed on Jews, not only because their numbers were smaller, but many Jews shared anti-Christian sentiments in the wake of the expulsion of the Jews from Spain in 1492. This policy created long-lasting animosity in many of the Jewish communities outside Europe, and found covert support in many European Jewish enclaves for Ottoman ambitions.

As a result of such stringent limitations being put upon them, a significant number of both Nestorian and Orthodox, and later, after the Ottoman conquest of the Egyptian Mameluke Empire, Coptic Christians retreated from major Ottoman cities and chose to live in small districts either in the country or in out-of-the-way towns, where they would draw less official attention to themselves. This made it possible for the Christians to avoid the consequences of keeping their religion, but it also tended to create a kind of social invisibility for Christians—and some groups of Jews as well—so that the Ottoman policy of tolerance for the Christian religion in all its forms was rarely put to the test.

There was also a significant minority of Zoroastrians, mostly in Persia, who were not so well tolerated as the Christians and Jews—not being People of The Book—and who therefore practiced their faith much more discreetly. They were not allowed to hold official posts; if they were slaves, they could not, themselves, own non-Islamic slaves as Islamic slaves could; they were prohibited from dealing with non-Islamic and non-Zoroastrian merchants; and they were required to pay double taxes on their property and their livestock as well, and to subject their young men to an annual draft into the Ottoman armies.

The friction among the Christian West and the Islamic East was as much economic as cultural, the latter being the more obvious, but the former more far-reaching, reflecting a shift in the movement of wealth in Europe and the Middle East. Since the fall of Rome, roughly a thousand years earlier, the movement of wealth in that vast region had been from West to East. After Lepanto, the pendulum swung back the other way, and wealth began to flow from East to West, a pattern that, in spite of the price of oil, continues to this day, although less comprehensively than was the case a century ago.

One of the reasons for that shift may have been that the Ottoman economy was a slave-based, or labor-based, economy, while the European economy was increasingly mercantile, another may have been the increasing social fluidity in the West, compared to the increasing social rigidity in the East; when it comes to economic advantage, money provides the most leverage of any exchange, and mercantilism is much more money-based than slave labor. The balance of power in the Middle East, based on traditional tribal and clan alliances, was often far more unstable internally than the more obviously tumultuous West. These differences of cultural style were often misunderstood by the various opponents, resulting in many miscalculations which served only to worsen the diplomatic stalemate, and pushed the conflict into concerted war instead of opportunistic predation: present-day patterns are not significantly improved.

Crucial to the socio-economic evolution of the sixteenth century was the European trump card—wealth from the New World which was adding so many treasuries in western Europe, principally to the already rich empire controlled by Spain, not only enabling a wide-scale defense of western shipping, but financing the more aggressive counter-measures that culminated in Lepanto. However, the New World also spread Spanish forces over much vaster territory than had ever been the case before, and that caused an already cautious administration to become even more reluctant to undertake skirmish naval warfare—which had been the usual pattern for two centuries—in favor of massive, concentrated attacks, like Lepanto.

Pressure from the Ottoman Empire was not the only major concern of the time for Europe: there were very real problems much closer to home, serving not only to divide populations, but to bring about a level of turmoil that disrupted cities and towns, commerce and finance. The sixteenth century was filled with religious ferment in Europe, marked by the rise of all manner of Protestantism from England to Poland to Sicily; the more diverse Protestantism became, the more dogmatic Catholicism turned in response, until the whole of European Christianity was dangerously polarized.

The politics compounded the religious problems: Germany, or more properly, the German States of the Holy Roman Empire, was a collection of kingdoms, duchies, counties, palatinates, bishoprics, and principalities that were further fractured by the shifting fortunes of Church and State, and this internal strife at first prevented any significant German participation in the resistance to the Ottoman expansion, a policy that cost the Austrian Hapsburgs dearly in their attempts to stem the overland tide from Constantinople, and prolonged the active military campaign on land for at least sixty years.

By contrast to the chaotic German states, Spain was easily the most cohesive—read: repressive—and affluent country in Europe at the time, and this gave it a significant advantage in its dealings with other nations, and, for that matter, the Catholic Church, which it strove to direct along its own, very conservative, path. Spanish-sponsored explorations were beginning to make an impact from the Far East to the Americas, creating a world-spanning commercial hegemony that accompanied a policy of colonization maintained along very strict lines that were rarely successfully challenged.

In addition to being wealthy and globally influential, Spain was one of the most politically and religiously conservative societies in Europe: while a great portion of Europe was caught up in the twin turbulence of the Renaissance and the Reformation, Spain rigorously eschewed both, preferring (in the name of Christian superiority) to stamp out all traces of change rather than tolerate them, at least at home. For this was the height of the power of the Spanish Inquisition, an institution that defined most of the policies of the Spanish Empire, and where Spain went, so did the Spanish version of Catholicism, carried by hosts of monks whose task it was to convert the heathen in foreign lands, or let the soldiers either enslave or kill them for being unworthy of salvation.

About five years before Lepanto, Felipe II appointed a Royal Commission to determine the savability of the natives of America: the Commission decided that since there was no mention of the American natives in Scripture, they were destined for Limbo and could not hope for Heaven, which meant that the Church need not be responsible for their salvation, or their abuse. For the next fifty years, this posture dictated Spanish policy toward all American natives with the sole exception of the Incas.

This absolutist mentality was not limited to religion, but extended itself into all aspects of life, particularly gender-based issues—they shared venomous misogyny with Islamic precepts of the period—and as a result, lay heavily on the Spanish people, permeating nearly all the diplomatic dealings Spain had with other countries, as well as leading to clashes with and among its own allies. In Spain, the persecution of supposed heretics reached levels significantly in excess of those in other countries, and served to feed the witch-frenzy in many

Protestant regions. It may be significant that in Spain, the accused heretics were, in nine out of ten cases, women, and it was regarded as proof of female diabolism if an Inquisitor got an erection during the Questioning (read: unofficial torture) of an accused woman.

Had Spain been more amenable to compromise of a diplomatic nature, the Turkish naval advancement might have been curtailed two or three decades earlier, and many losses of life, land, and goods have been averted. But since Spain had undergone almost six centuries of Moorish occupation of the southern half of the Iberian peninsula and any concession to Islamic forces was seen as an invitation to the Moors to return, such a solution was deemed impossible from the start. Those Europeans questioning the Spanish obduracy went unheeded at best, or religiously persecuted at worst.

There were clashes within the Ottoman ranks, as well, but they were less visible, and were often treated privately—through bribery, assassination, isolation, family persuasion, or combinations of any and all of these. The court of the Ottoman Sultan was known to be a morass of intrigue and skulduggery, but with a united cultural purpose and religious singleness of intent beyond the politics of influence and advancement; that sense of dual aim was usually sufficient to override personal commitments, such as generations-long vendettas and internal feuds, but there was always a hint of interior machinations within the larger diplomatic dealings. This style of handling things was reflected throughout the military as well: there were a number of captains associated with the Ottoman navy who were little better than pirates—the dreaded corsairs, whose predations on European merchant vessels had created havoc from the eastern Atlantic to Trebizond.

Not that the Holy League did not have some questionable leaders as well, for many of the independent captains on land and sea had highly equivocal reputations, and pasts that would not bear close scrutiny. Because of the Church's intense involvement in the Holy

League, there was an attempt to present at least the appearance of respectability, if not piety, so the jealousies and bickering of the military leaders of the Holy League were represented as the acts of courageous men of high mettle and unassailable honor instead of the vanity and arrogance they actually were. Add to that the promise of plunder—many of those who answered the call to battle saw treasure as their reward instead of redemption.

In many ways, Lepanto was an act of desperation for the Europeans, only agreed to at the instigation of the Pope as a last-ditch effort; the various rulers were too wary of one another to undertake such an enterprise without the imprimatur of Papal approval, and rivalries within the Holy League were intense. The Ottoman forces were larger, and much more confident. On both sides the various leaders were intensely competitive with one another. Both the Holy League and the Ottoman forces had a great deal riding on this conflict and neither side could support maintaining a large navy at full preparedness for very long, which lent urgency to the engagement. Men on both sides were determined to stop the other side, and had the assurance that God would aid them in the fight. Numbers alone gave the advantage to the Ottoman forces. But the Holy League—in particular, the Venetians—had one, minor technical advantage in their ships' design that, in this battle, proved crucial to the outcome.

By the time the two navies met in the Gulf of Lepanto, the battle was a grudge match. There was a long history of violence and treachery behind all the forces in this engagement; feelings were running high, and each side was convinced that God would give them the victory because their opponents were so egregious in every way. Both sides had men at their oars who had been captured during skirmishes with the other side, and that meant that on the Ottoman ships there were oarsmen hoping the Ottomans would fail, and on the Holy League ships there were captured Turks chained to oars who were supporting the Ottoman navy, not the European one. Although both sides loudly declared their unity of purpose, and the necessity to settle matters once and for all, the situation was more complicated than that. Neither side was as unified as it claimed to be, and most of the combatants had secondary agendas attached to the outcome of the campaign as well as their obvious military and political objectives.

One of the reasons for this insistence on the appearance of mono-lithic resolve was the religious element in the confrontation, for the politics of faith informed every aspect of the long struggle that culmi-nated at Lepanto. While this was hardly a new situation in war—almost all armies and navies have been assured that they fight for a righteous cause as well as the right to loot—due to the exacerbated state of specifically religious hostility between these forces, the rancor was unusually acute, the stakes were higher because of it, and the fighting itself more bitter.

To understand the depth of the conflict, it is useful to understand its origins, and the origins of the forces who fought it, for this was a battle brought about not simply by religio-socio-commercial growing pains, but by centuries of cumulative mutual injuries that resulted in a partic-ularly bloody one-upmanship in which every aspect of the battle had ties to past insults; for these reasons, the outcome would echo for cen-turies more.

2

THE OTTOMAN EMPIRE

UNTIL THE MID-700S A.D. there were two groups of Turks living in Central Asia: the Western Turks, in and around what is now Kazakhstan and Turkestan, and the Celestial Turks, living in central and western Mongolia, to the south of Lake Baikal; they were probably called Celestial because of the frequency of blue eyes in the population—it was certainly not because they were virtuous and high-minded, or even unworldly, for the region was harsh and their lives were arduous, competitive, and rarely more than at the subsistence level for the vast majority of the population. The Turks had achieved a kind of workable-if-belligerent stasis with the other peoples of their regions, and although occupying a central place in the multi-cultural territories, the Turks often endured skirmish warfare and livestock raids from their neighbors, which they answered in kind.

Nomadic, preliterate, and contentious, the various Turkish clans began a westward migration around A.D. 750, for reasons that are still debated, but are likely connected to two long famines recorded in China in the 720s (three years) and 730s (two years), and the subsequent pressure of other, more northern, tribes moving down into what had been exclusively Turkish territory and settling in it with their families and herds. The Turks were overwhelmed by this steady tide, and began their migration, visiting what had been their fate on the peoples who stood in their way as they abandoned their homeland for an uncertain future in the Middle East.

This westward migration was not at first an organized march in a vast body, such as many of the Huns had made some centuries earlier, but for the most part a matter of a clan or small group of clans going beyond traditional territory into new places where they could feed their camels, sheep, and goats without too much competition, holding this new territory as their own, and then, in a generation or so, moving westward again, pushing the native groups ahead of them or subsuming them into their numbers either as slaves or as mercenaries or as concubines, moving inexorably toward the Mediterranean Basin in a journey that would take more than three centuries to complete in consequential numbers. As a result, the Turks moved westward on many roads, following either trade routes or grazing tracks, usually choosing the least hostile area to cross. Most of their travels were intended to be as peaceable as possible—the Turks not having sufficient numbers or materiel for a major military campaign—but if they encountered opposition, they fought to gain and hold territory, at least for the first few centuries of their migration.

Only when a significant presence had been established in Asia Minor did the trickle become a flood, and the Turks, who had taken over Persia as part of their westward expansion, extended the substance of their interests farther westward into the Byzantine Empire. Once they achieved something more than a toehold in Anatolia, their numbers increased suddenly and dramatically as a steady wave of Turks advanced in ever more organized and ever larger groups, duplicating the methods that had secured Persia for them.

During their migrations, as Turks traveled into southern Russia and northern Persia, large numbers of their clans converted to Islam, so that by the time they reached Anatolia, most of them were coreligionists with the vast majority of the peoples living around them, and therefore they were marginally more welcome than they might have been otherwise. The commonality of Islam limited the kind of excesses that could be committed upon one another—at least in theological expectation. The Turks also had the considerable advantage of ties reaching all the way back to Mongolia, which eased eastern trade for many Turkish merchants, and built wealth for what would become the Ottoman Empire through its many ports and trade-route connections. From the tenth century on, Turks controlled a number of crucial trade routes, most particularly the western end of the Silk Road, the ancient trade route between China and the Mediterranean, and through that mercantile hegemony, the Ottoman Empire financed the first stages of its major expansion.

For more than a century, at the beginnings of the Ottoman Empire, the Turks were willing to act as interface for the Mediterranean merchants trading with the Far East through Black Sea ports, profiting from customs and transference fees as well as a tradition of price-fixing and pilferage that touched all the commerce in which they participated, which reflected the conduct of most European merchants when they had opportunity for such exploitation. This ongoing profiteering lessened when the Crusades began, for until that time, the Turkish relationship with Europe had been fairly untrammeled, but as Crusaders invaded their territory, practicing havoc on their way to defend the Holy Land, the Turks—and the Christian Greeks—became hostile to the rampaging Europeans.

By the end of the thirteenth century, as the crusading zeal was finally beginning to fade in Europe, the Turks were established throughout most of what is modern-day Turkey, and held positions of considerable clout. They made themselves indispensable by supporting the Islamic forces against European Crusaders and the beleaguered Byzantine Greeks, whose Empire had been fatally weakened by battles with the Latin west in the thirteenth century, and although maintaining the facade of invulnerability, was crumbling internally. By taking on the Byzantine Greeks, the Ottomans staked out their future territory, and proved their worth in the region by helping to contain the Mongol invasions moving along the same routes the Turks themselves had traveled four centuries earlier. Mongol adventurism culminated in the vast empire of Jenghiz Khan, which eventually saw Hulegu, the marginally Buddhist grandson of Jenghiz Khan and brother of the emperor of China, Kublai Khan, whose mother had been a Nestorian Christian, ruling in Baghdad and endorsing, if not actually embracing, the precepts of Islam.

As a capstone to the Turkish presence, in 1290 the Bithynian king, a Seljuk Turk named Osman al-Ghazi, a very capable leader with great ambitions, and, according to legend, blue-eyed and therefore fortunate, having succeeded his father Ertogrul two years before, founded his empire at Osmanli, the name from which Ottoman is derived. Osman ruled until 1326—a considerable reign for those times, when the average life-expectancy for the upper-class male was between thirty-two and thirty-eight—expanding his territory throughout most of his long reign. The forces he set in motion continued long after Osman's death. Expansionism was a cornerstone of Ottoman policy that marked the next three and a half centuries.

As conflict with the Christian Byzantines intensified, the Turks became more important, for they were in a good geographic position to push the Greeks back and to maintain control of the land the Byzantines had been compelled to abandon. Hardy travelers and dedicated warriors, the Turks kept the pressure on the Greeks at as many points as possible, wearing away at the weakest places along the frontier of Byzantine territory until resistance broke, and the Turks could occupy that portion of formerly Byzantine land and use it as a position from which to press the Greeks back again.

To thwart European trade and turn trading to their advantage, they became adept sailors, working with the Greeks, Arabs, Phoenicians, and Syrians to improve their ships in design and armament, and began what was to be a centuries-long campaign of harrying and piracy at sea. This was aimed primarily at the early medieval trading giants of Venice and Genoa, whose commercial ventures were sending ships to ports on the Black Sea and the Sea of Azov, and all the way into the Atlantic to trade with the Hanseatic League in Antwerp and Hamburg, and with English merchants in London.

For three centuries the merchants and the Turks maintained an uneasy but mutually beneficial state of balance based on shared convenience and joint economic advantage, marked by occasional skirmishes on sea and land, but nothing so extreme that open warfare resulted. But as time went by and power centers shifted, the political and religious climate changed, and the mutual advantage that existed prior to the Crusades gave way to exploitation so that military and economic pressure began to weigh heavily on the European merchants trading in Ottoman territory.

Soon the Turks were at the forefront of the drive to get Constantinople into Islamic hands. Turks now occupied positions of real power beyond their own regions as Ottoman influence increased, with Turks rising to prominence in a culture that had evolved to accommodate their heritage as well as the traditions and customs of the established societal and religious groups. Turkish interests became intrinsic to the Islamic advance, and as a result, the Turks spearheaded the advance on Byzantine territory, and benefited from the campaign and its outcome.

A quarter century after the fall of Constantinople, in January of 1479, the Turks concluded a treaty with the Venetians which in theory protected the Venetians' rights to trade in Ottoman territory—at the cost of 10,000 Venetian ducats a year (a ducat being a coin minted from 3.5 grams of gold) and some territorial concessions at the far edges of the Venetian empire. Also in theory this made continuing dealings between the Venetian and Ottoman empires an ongoing and equitable arrangement, but in practice matters turned out very differently.

It was shortly after the fall of Constantinople that the Ottoman ambassador remarked to a high-ranking Venetian that in a while the

Ottoman Sultan and not the Venetian Doge would annually marry the Adriatic Sea. (The Venetian Doge was rowed out every spring in the state barge to drop a gold ring into the water to symbolize Venice's continuing union with the sea.) This attitude continued to grow in the Ottoman diplomatic dealings with Europe. Tensions heightened steadily, adding incentives to New World exploration as Europeans sought supposed Asian goods and markets far from the greed and caprice of the Ottoman officials whose capacity for graft, once initiated, seemed insatiable. That the Venetians were willing to pay exorbitant bribes in order to secure advantageous arrangements for themselves over other European traders only served to exacerbate an already corrupt system.

As an indication of the growing precariousness of the situation, the treaty with Venice was difficult to enforce because the Ottoman Sultan could not and would not be responsible for the actions of the supposedly independent corsairs, who continued to pursue European merchant ships with unabashed, gleeful ferocity; they had no incentive not to, for they kept all but ten percent of their loot and were not considered criminals so long as they did not attack Islamic ships. This provided the Sultan an excellent excuse to look the other way when European ships were seized, a stance that hit hardest at the Venetians, who were paying handsomely for a level of safety that was at best theoretical. This two-tiered policy, one which kept the Ottoman navy in check but gave free rein to the corsairs, served to speed the deterioration of Ottoman-European relations.

About all the treaty actually guaranteed the Venetians in practice was that their ships, cargoes, and crews would not be confiscated in Ottoman ports, and, less certainly, that their island possessions in the Mediterranean, Adriatic, and Aegean Seas would not be attacked and taken over by Ottoman forces. It wasn't much, but the Venetians at the time were in no position to haggle—a bad deal was better than no deal at all.

None of these bargains were so binding that they could endure the vicissitudes of trade, and the Venetian Empire began to lose ground as the Byzantines had done. Pragmatic as the Venetians were, they knew they could not sustain continuing skirmishes with the Turks, nor could they afford all-out war and the resultant loss of many markets, and so they redoubled their diplomatic efforts, but with little real success: the Turks were on a roll and determined to make the most of it.

By 1530, the Ottoman Empire had annexed the Egyptian-based Mameluke Empire, and thus gained control over the entire eastern end of the Mediterranean, turning the Ottoman warships, which had in effect doubled in numbers with the acquisition of the Mameluke fleet, into the largest deployed navy in the Mediterranean Basin; on top of that, the Sultan ordered an increase in warship production to enlarge the navy still further. At the same time, Ottoman forces had acquired over twenty safe harbors for their ships, thus assuring that the Ottoman navy would continue to be the most powerful naval presence in the Mediterranean Basin by virtue of having so many ports where Ottoman ships could be protected. It was a state of affairs that the Europeans—particularly the Venetians—could not allow to continue unchallenged indefinitely without risking complete economic and military collapse.

In response to this predicament, the Venetians stepped up their production of warships and seriously looked for ways to gain any sort of advantage over the swift, maneuverable corsairs' ships. By 1569, they had that one advantage they had sought, and it was new enough to their ships that the Ottoman navy had not yet found a way to counter it—in fact, its importance went largely unnoticed by the corsairs until after Lepanto, where its efficacy was demonstrated beyond all cavil.

Naval strategies were much the same for the European and Ottoman navies, but the corsairs were another matter. Corsairs usually hunted in groups of three or four fast ships; most corsairs preferred the galliot, a kind of light war galley, smaller than a galley and more maneuverable. They would stalk a flotilla of merchant vessels, choosing which of the ships was most promising; they would cut out a single European merchant ship—usually the most heavily laden, not only because it promised the richest treasure, but because it was apt to be the slowest—from the group of vessels that sailed together, with two, and occasionally three, corsair ships crossing the merchant ship's bow, then flanking and boarding the merchant craft so that the corsairs could not only seize the ship and its cargo, but its crew and oarsmen could be taken as slaves and any passengers held for ransom. The tactics are not unlike those used by the German submarines hunting cargo-vessels under military escort in World War II, except that the submarines were in no position to board the merchant ships, and looting was, at best, impracticable.

It was usually difficult or impossible for accompanying merchant ships or their escorts to come to the rescue of a doomed galley, because there was a great risk of becoming an additional victim of the corsairs, the merchant ships being neither as fast nor as maneuverable as the corsairs', and lacking many trained soldiers to fight the Ottomans. Most sailors and oarsmen understood that if they became the target of corsairs, they stood a very poor chance of being rescued. The escort war galleys rarely had the opportunity to engage the corsairs before they had fixed on their target merchant ship because that exposed other merchant ships to the corsairs. The few soldiers on the merchant ships were more cosmetic than effective. The intervention of war galleys in this kind of battle did not spare the merchant ship, and often risked adding the protective war galley, its crew, soldiers, and weapons, to the corsairs' bounty.

For a while almost all of the European trading city-states provided increased numbers of military ships as escorts for their merchants, but this proved to be too costly in men and materiel, for, as noted, the corsairs soon developed their skills and would capture the military ships, their weapons, and their soldiers and oarsmen, taking over the ships and weapons, then selling the captured men as slaves as well as profiting from the cargo of the merchant ships.

The Venetians finally realized that the only way to defeat the corsairs consistently was to keep them at a distance, and to that end, began to use heavier cannon and to build the decks of the war galleys roughly a foot higher than the decks of the Ottoman ships. It may not seem like much, but the slightly heavier cannon and the higher decks meant that the Venetian ships could hold off just out of reach of the Ottoman cannon and either pound the corsairs' ships to matchwood, or soften them up enough to cause them to retreat. If the corsairs could not be forced to abandon their aggression, then the barrage would attempt to damage them so that they had to attack at less than full strength, thus postponing the point of the disastrous close-combat boardings of the past, where the more maneuverable Ottoman ships had the advantage. Without these two apparently minor improvements, the outcome of Lepanto would have been markedly different.

Traditional naval warfare of the period was based on the strategy that whenever possible, both sides would disable their opponents, then grapple and tow the battered foe to the first safe harbor; this would allow the victors to loot the ship for any treasure, weapons, or munitions on board, and to free the men chained to the oars, for in most instances, more than half of them had been taken by other captains in other battles, and would welcome being restored to their own sides in this long, increasingly devastating unofficial war.

As cannon improved, becoming more reliable and more accurate—and less likely to explode when hot—and the number of them on each European ship increased, the potential of artillery fire exceeded the utility of Greek fire (not the Greek fire of ancient times, but a combination of crude oil and matted lint that was good for setting decks and sails aflame, but nowhere near as devastating as the original Greek fire had been) and flaming arrows—until then, the preferred weapons of the Turks. The corsairs were forced to give up a little of their speed and maneuverability for heavier ships capable of surviving cannon fire, lessons that were driven home at Lepanto.

3

THE VENETIANS

URING THE BEGINNING years of the Dark Ages (roughly
A.D. 400–500), the peoples of what is now northeastern
Italy found themselves under waves of attack from various barbarian
invaders on their way from eastern Europe and the Asian steppes to
sack Rome: Goths, Lombards, Alans, Avars, Huns, and many lesser
groups came through the Balkans and the Alps, headed south down
the Italian peninsula, raiding, pillaging, and killing as they went, or,
in the case of the Vandals, came up through Italy from the south,
headed for the Danube Valley, and eventually, to the broad grasslands
of what is now Poland, Vandalizing as they went.

For those who made their living on the fertile, forested plain and
rolling hills between the Po River and the north end of the Adriatic
Sea, these ongoing invasions became too calamitous to resist; continuing to live on the mainland under such conditions was dangerous
and impracticable, so in order to protect themselves from raids and
worse, the people of the region gradually retreated onto the islands of
the lagoon at the northern end of the Adriatic Sea, reinforcing the
low-lying, marshy islands with deeply sunk logs which were driven
down through the soft earth and mud to as firm a footing as they
could reach in order to provide a foundation for their first, and
all subsequent, buildings. Even today, Venice stands on a forest of
sunken logs.

Starting from the island of Murano, now famous for its beautiful

glass-making and even in the early days of Venice a center of European glass production, these determined survivors expanded their
occupation to other islands in the lagoon, taking down tens of thousands of trees to provide a footing for their burgeoning settlement.
They took apart their major buildings, ferried them out to the island,
and rebuilt them even while they constructed their first houses. Next
they banned horses from the islands, and started to develop all manner of shallow-draft boats to carry goods from the mainland to the
city in the sea, for there was insufficient open land available on the islands to do any significant farming, and too much salt in the water to
allow most regular crops to grow on the islands, had there been room
to grow them.

Thus, although protected by the sea, the Venetians were also
maintaining a precarious balance on their carefully constructed islands, with almost all foodstuffs and fresh water obtained from the
mainland. With the exception of fish, which, perforce, formed the
base of the Venetian diet, food came entirely from mainland sources
well into the sixteenth century, and this, for all practical purposes,
continues to this day. Venice, in saving its people from the constant
risk of assault, subjected them to the hazards of perpetual reprovi-
sioning. This dependence on shipped-in food and goods was a continuing peril that acted very early in the city's existence to spur the
Venetians into regional commerce, for not only was their location
highly advantageous for developing maritime trade, the need for
ready money—in this case, Venetian ducats—to pay for the necessar-
ily imported food and other supplies was paramount in maintaining
the growing population of the cluster of islands.

Beginning with the salt trade with inland towns, then branching
out into spices obtained from Arabian and Egyptian merchants, the
Venetians quickly expanded their ventures and their range of ports-
of-call, so that by the time of the Crusades they had become a true
commercial superpower, and were able to take advantage of their

wide-range trading. Their position, geographically and financially, made them the most important center for sea transport to the Holy Land, and the Venetians added to their wealth by carrying soldiers, horses, materiel, and weapons to the various Crusaders' ports and fortresses along the eastern shores of the Mediterranean, enterprises that not only added to Venetian coffers but extended markets and merchandise for the Most Serene Republic.

With an increased European military presence in the Middle East, Venice was in an ideal location to exploit the western end of the major Eurasian trade routes, as well as expanding their European ports-of-call, increasing their general importance in the commercial ties of East to West; by 1000, Venice had established outposts at Tana, on the Sea of Azov; at Trapezus (Trebizond), Sinope, Kaffa, and Constantinople in the Black Sea; in Lisbon, Bruges, Antwerp, Southampton, and London, for Atlantic Ocean and North Sea trade. Closer to home, they had commercial missions on Corfu, Rhodes, and Cyprus (which became part of the Venetian empire and was crucial to the Lepanto campaign) in Greece; in Zara on the Dalmatian coast; in Tripoli and Beirut in Syria; in Alexandria, Tripoli, Tunis, Bône, Bougie, Algiers, Oran, and Melilla in Africa; also in the European centers of Messina, Palermo, Naples, Civitavecchia, Pisa (when they were not at war), Toulon, Marseilles, Aigues-Mortes, Barcelona, Valencia, Almeria, Malaga, and Cadiz.

These shipping routes, known as galleys, were regularized after the Crusades, and were the mainstay of Venetian wealth for more than three centuries prior to Lepanto as the adventuresome traders continued to expand their mercantilism. Their success is easily demonstrable: Venetian ducats have been found all through northern Africa, in southern Russia, in eastern Europe and the Slavic states, in the Balkans and Carpathians, throughout the Arabian peninsula, all along the Silk Road, in Acapulco, Vera Cruz, Santo Domingo, and San Salvador, and as far away as eastern China and central India. In a time when the average man rarely traveled more than thirty miles from the place of his birth, the Venetian ducat may have been the most-traveled coin of the medieval and Renaissance worlds.

The Venetian Empire was defined by an explosive mix of trade and politics, the Venetian Republic founded on principles of exchange and enlarging markets. More than the Genoese, who were under the combined influence of Spain and, after A.D. 900, France, the Venetians were in a position, financially and geographically, that gave them more independence than many seagoing mercantile states enjoyed a thousand years ago. By establishing their own empire, the Venetians decreased the likelihood of their annexation to other kingdoms. The Alps held the Germans at bay, and the Lombards in central Italy had come under the rule of the fledgling Holy Roman Empire, and so were not overly concerned with a group of islands at the north end of the Adriatic, thus ensuring that Venice would be able to go its own way in the world largely unhampered by its neighbors. Venice became a buffer to the Italian peninsula against the rambunctious tribes to the east, and as such was valued highly by Dark Age Italy.

By the time the Papal States were truly secure, Venice was too well-established to be bullied into confederation with the hodgepodge of Italian states, although the Venetian Empire actively pursued a course of good diplomatic relations with all its Italian neighbors, especially the Papal States, since these were its principal European markets. Through it all, the Venetians remained the most Byzantine of Italian societies. Even the Venetian brand of Catholicism had an Eastern Orthodox influence—the reigning archbishop was officially called the Patriarch of Venice, in the Orthodox tradition, and Saint Mark's Basilica has a strong Byzantine flavor to its design—that came out of the extensive contact the Venetians had with Eastern Christianity, as well as the occasional spates of refugees arriving in Venice over the centuries from Orthodox territory as the

Ottoman Empire began its competitive expansion. There was even a small Greek Orthodox church in Venice, on the Giudecca, until the late 1600s.

Ruled by elected Doges (from the Latin *dux,* meaning leader) who were advised by the Minor Consiglio (cabinet, sometimes called the Council of Ten, which actually by the end of the sixteenth century consisted of Seventeen), and governed by the Maggior Consiglio (Grand Council, or the Venetian Senate, which eventually numbered about 1,500 members), Venice was, in a limited sense, a democracy. (Throughout most of the Republic's history, free Catholic males of legal age owning property and/or ships on which they paid taxes could vote.) The Venetians protected their Republic fiercely even as they kept up ruthless competition for positions of power within it; a dozen or so families came to dominate Venetian government for almost eight hundred years.

The Venetians did not often attempt to force their style of government on the non-Venetians in their empire, although they welcomed various representatives from their client countries to participate in their version of democracy, and encouraged more representative governments in parts of their empire where such regimes would be advantageous to Venetian interests.

More than most Europeans, the Venetians appreciated the problems of maintaining a far-flung empire, particularly by sea, and did their best to balance their ambitions without biting off more than they could chew. Whenever possible, they conducted their external politics the same way they handled their business contracts—with money. They much preferred to buy territory than to go to war for it, since war was usually bad for business. Although they maintained a well-armed navy, they did not often undertake a military offensive when a diplomatic or commercial one would do as well. On the other hand, if they were compelled to fight, they were as ruthless as any medieval fighting force, and that gained them the grudging respect of most of their partner cities in trade. So long as the Venetian government grasped the problems the Most Serene Republic confronted, their methods tended to be successful. But astute leadership was not always the mark of the elected Doges, and from time to time, that made for real trouble.

In 1570, the largely ineffective Doge Pietro Loredan was succeeded by Alvise Mocenigo, the first of four Doges of that name—Alvise Mocenigo II (ruled 1700–1709), III (ruled 1722–1732), and IV (ruled 1763–1778)—from a rich and influential family that had given the Venetian Republic three previous Doges: Tommaso (ruled 1414–1423), Pietro (ruled 1474–1476), and Giovanni (ruled 1478–1485). With such a family background, it is not surprising that Alvise Mocenigo I (ruled 1570–1577) was keenly aware of the danger Venice faced from Ottoman aggression, and he was unwilling to concede anything more to the Sultan than had already been granted, preferably without having to resort to open warfare, which was inevitably bad for business.

Yet Alvise I was also a pragmatist, and knew that Ottoman demands for Venetian territory were only going to increase; shortly before his death, Doge Pietro Loredan had refused the Sultan's ambassador's ships permission to dock at Venice, aware that the ambassador could have no purpose other than to demand that the Venetians hand over more of their territory, and to demonstrate the Ottoman capability of going where they liked, when they liked. The next day when the ambassador was allowed to land, he was met by a contingent of armed soldiers who escorted him to the Signoria for what turned out to be a very brief meeting, at which the Ottoman ambassador was informed that the Maggior Consiglio had voted not to surrender Cyprus, which was a de facto declaration of war.

Doge Loredan's pettiness—snide by Venetian standards, but unpardonably offensive to an Ottoman official—only fueled Ottoman resentment and fanned the ambitions of the Turks; they were already expanding into Bulgaria, Romania, Bosnia, Serbia, and Hungary, and had indicated an interest in claiming more Venetian territory along the Dalmatian coast, a threat the Consiglio took very seriously. Alvise I realized that Venice could not fight this particular war alone, and so began his Dogeship with the careful diplomatic pursuit of European allies, keeping in mind as he did that Europe had other problems on its plate and that many of the European states had become accustomed to letting Venice and Genoa take care of the corsairs without needing much help from other naval powers.

While it was true that the great maritime republics of Venice and Genoa had taken the brunt of Ottoman naval aggression, their own six-hundred-year-old strife made it difficult for the two Italian merchant-states to act in concert even as the Turkish corsairs stepped up their attacks on European merchant ships. Venice, which despite losses to its empire still maintained control over several of the Greek islands and a section of the Dalmatian coast, was most seriously damaged by the escalating hostilities with the Ottoman Empire, for the Venetians not only relied upon the spice and dye trades more heavily than Genoa, they operated more extensively in the eastern Mediterranean, the Adriatic, Aegean, and Black Seas than the Genoese did, and maintained more outposts on Greek islands.

But in spite of the thriving spice markets in Europe, for several centuries the Most Serene Republic had been left to fend for herself in her battles with the Ottomans. Genoa not only benefited from Venice's losses, which opened markets for them, but since it was part of the Spanish hegemony, it was not as dependent on eastern trade as Venice was, and as such was not inclined to act against the Turks without the specific sanction of the Spanish crown. The Spanish were reluctant to give this for historical as well as immediate reasons: the hope of gaining access to Asia through the New World was becoming a reality—although a more complex one than first assumed, for crossing the Americas to reach the Pacific and Asia beyond was a venture of several years' duration; the Genoese were often employed by the Spanish to man their long-distance voyages. As much as Genoa wanted access to eastern Mediterranean ports, it wanted Spanish goodwill more, so over time Genoese trade with Ottoman ports decreased, with the exception of North African ports, leaving Venice even more isolated in the ongoing attempts to block Ottoman expansion, a challenge that Venice met with intensified reliance on superior ships.

The Arsenal, Venice's great ship-building establishment, was aware of the advantages of standardization, and by the middle of the 1540s, they had developed a uniform design for war galleys—and other ships as well—which allowed them to produce the galleys quickly from pre-cut parts, an improvement in manufacturing that meant also that the crews and soldiers could be moved from war galley to war galley without having to learn anything new about the ships.

The decks of Venetian war galleys in the second half of the sixteenth century were 137.5 feet long, 22.5 feet abeam, plus the outrigger for the oarsmen and their oars. The galleys drew nine feet when stocked and manned. The slight raising of the deck was incorporated into the ships' construction in 1569, and resulted in an equally slight lengthening (to 139.8 feet) and broadening (to 24.2 feet) of the main deck, and somewhat more reinforcement beneath the deck to accommodate the increase in cannon—depending on the amount of deck needed for soldiers, the number of cannon varied from thirty-five to fifty—and the additional stress of the oarsmen's outriggers, but did not change the actual length of the keel of the ship. Rigged with lateen sails and guided by a stern-mounted rudder—an adaptation of an earlier corsair design—the sixteenth-century Venetian merchant galley had a load capacity of approximately 600 tons, a tripling of capacity over a period of two centuries.

The Venetians traditionally kept a hundred war galleys ready-made in reserve, so if ships were lost, the fleet itself was not diminished, and new ships could be put into service at once, with little or no shake-down time for the crews, thanks to the standardized design. Over time, this reserve became, in actuality, a kind of mothball fleet, more for show than for use, circumstances that changed abruptly in 1499, when production went into high gear and remained high for a century.

The Arsenal produced ships on a production-line basis, putting everything but the oarsmen and sailors on the ship by the time it was finished. All parts of the ship, from sails to keel, were made at the Arsenal, the sails sewn there by four hundred seamstresses, the iron-work done by a hundred blacksmiths. The Arsenal was so important to Venice that five hundred thousand ducats of its seven-million-ducat annual state budget was provided to the Arsenal, and more than one job in four in the city was tied, directly or indirectly, to the Arsenal. No other naval power could produce ships of the quality, or at the speed, that the Venetians could, and no other naval power was so habitually prepared for conflict that it kept up the production of war galleys whether it was officially at peace or not.

For Venice, national policy was usually aimed at keeping away from active military engagements whenever possible. As this became more an ideal than a fact, the Venetians still did their utmost to disrupt trade as little as they could, carrying on commercial and diplomatic enterprises throughout Ottoman territory until such ventures proved to be too risky, at which point the Venetians took a more assertive posture in regard to their commerce, and changed their methods of guarding their trading ships.

Galleys, both merchant ships and war galleys, were at the heart of Venetian commerce. As Ottoman corsairs stepped up their attacks, the Venetians increased the size of their sailing groups, so that from 1400 to 1550, the number of ships in trade-route fleets grew until they were as large as the entire navies of smaller city-states. This not only protected them, it made them greater targets, leading to an escalation in the number of war galleys needed to protect the merchant fleets, which brought more corsairs into the hunt, and meant more war galleys were needed, adding to the desirability of such prizes, because the merchants sent more ships with the larger military escorts, so that corsairs and the Ottoman navy grew larger . . . and so on in the familiar arms race spiral.

4

THE HAPSBURGS

EW RULING FAMILIES have left such a mark on Europe as the Hapsburgs (sometimes spelled Habsburgs). From their first rise to power in Austria in 1273, followed by the acquisition of Bohemia and Hungary, creating the Austro-Hungarian Empire which formed the basis of their ongoing ascendancy throughout Europe, the Hapsburgs made themselves synonymous with eastern European power for six centuries, and remained a force there much longer than in other parts of their far-flung empires. Given the Austrian vulnerability to Ottoman aggression on the southeastern flank of their territory, it is hardly surprising that Hapsburgs would be inclined to support all efforts to minimize the Turkish expansion, or that such an expansion would fall most heavily upon them. As Hapsburg interests broadened, as much through provident marriages as force of arms, so did their reasons for keeping the Ottoman Empire out of Europe, and as their stakes grew higher, the magnitude of the threat increased proportionately.

By 1452, when Frederick V of Germany was elected Holy Roman Emperor Frederick III, the Hapsburg family gained the title and influence that would remain with them until the end of the Holy Roman Empire in 1806. Having achieved formidable regional power, Frederick's son, Maximillian I, in his marriage of 1477, gained Holland, Burgundy, Luxembourg, and through the various marriages of his descendants added the crowns of Spain, Sicily, Sardinia, Naples,

and a collection of duchies and principalities running from the North
Sea through the old Lorraine trade route to Avignon and Marseilles.
By the sixteenth century, the Hapsburgs were related by blood or
marriage to almost all the ruling Houses in Europe, and had diplomatic ties to some of the most important centers of the Ottoman
Empire, although such associations were defined by treaties, not by
marriage contracts.

Upon the death of Charles (Carlos) I of Spain (the grandson of
Ferdinand V of Castile and Leon, which is how the Austrian Hapsburgs came to rule Spain)—also known as the Holy Roman Emperor
Charles V—the Hapsburg holdings split, with the Spanish line de-
scending from Charles' son Philip (Felipe) II until 1700, and the
eastern European branch, later called Hapsburg-Lorraine, which was
centered in Austria, lasting there until 1918. The result of the split
was that the two branches of the family were at virtual cross-purposes
with each other, so the possibility of using these familial ties to miti-
gate this external threat was unlikely, and precious opportunities
were lost while the Hapsburgs wrangled internally.

This determined and capable family had a number of problems
besetting it in the second half of the sixteenth century, including two
religious policies that ran the gamut from arch-reactionary (in Spain)
to limited tolerance, given the nature of the time (in Austria). Hardest hit by this was the Netherlands, which was part of the Spanish
Hapsburg holdings, but whose people were far more like the subjects
of the Austrian branch of the family, Holland being a major center
of religious dissent and intellectual exploration, and therefore constantly at odds with Spanish religious goals, and subject to severe responses on the part of the Spanish authorities. The Austrian branch
of the family studiously avoided getting into confrontations with Spain
over Holland, a policy that made sense at the time, but which eventually worked against them, losing them both political and financial
clout in the region as the Dutch, driven by ruthless persecution by the

Spanish, finally gained independence from Spain and all things Hapsburg. The reluctance of the Austrian Hapsburgs to challenge their Spanish cousins, thanks to the rebellion in the Netherlands, created a host of problems in northern Europe that contributed to the Spanish incapacity to respond reasonably or effectively to the pressures of the Enlightenment, a century after Lepanto.

In the midst of decisive Ottoman attacks on eastern Hapsburg possessions, when unity was most needed, the Spanish resolve to wipe out heresy wherever it was found worked against the international strategies attempted by Charles I/V. After the death of Charles I/V, having no ruler or relative strong enough to oppose him, Felipe II, in 1567, sent troops to Antwerp to capture the city and execute the heretical leaders of the Dutch opposition, thus precipitating eighty years of war as the people of the Netherlands struggled to free themselves from Spain.

The Dutch were not the only people living under Spanish rule to be singled out for harsh treatment. The Islamic Moors had been expelled from Spain in 1492 by Isabella the Catholic, and the impact of that expulsion was still being felt in Spain almost a century later—as the Morisco Revolt of 1569 indicated, when a group of supposedly converted Moors strove to reestablish a Moorish region of Spain and through it to stop the policy of prejudicial taxation and asset-confiscation along with quasi-legal prosecutions for supposed apostasy. This made Spain inclined to avoid any head-on encounter with the Ottomans even while they tried to gain control of Islamic ports in northwestern Africa to prevent just the sort of piracy they saw expanding in the Adriatic and Black Seas. The lifting of the Siege of Malta—which was begun in May 1565 by the Ottoman navy against the Knights of Saint John, for whom the Ottomans had a special hatred—by Spanish reinforcements arriving in September, while atypical of Spanish policy, only served to make both sides of the conflict more obdurate.

This stalemate went on for almost fifty years, the Venetians still taking the main thrust of Turkish aggression and slowly but steadily losing ground to it, the Turks becoming bolder and richer with every passing decade. The Hapsburg territories were not encouraged to assist Venetian interests—for one thing, Venice's greatest rival, Genoa, was part of the Spanish sphere of influence, and there were good reasons not to appear to favor Venice over Genoa, particularly in military matters. Since the Venetians and the Genoese were traditional rivals and enemies, Spain was compelled by treaties to support the Genoese—a position that Spain found advantageous, for the Spanish had no good reason to waste energy, ships, and money keeping track of the Venetians at a time when their attention was turned on the New World.

This state of affairs between the Ottoman Empire and the West might have gone on for decades more, had there been no change in the pattern of Ottoman attacks, and no attempt to take Spanish treasure ships returning from the Americas. Attacking from African ports, the corsairs began to prey on Spanish ships with the same determination that they used to hunt Venetian merchant flotillas. In spite of many internal difficulties, the Spanish and Austrian Hapsburgs finally found something they could agree about, and that accord made the re-creation of the old medieval alliance—the so-called Holy League—possible.

Spanish Hapsburg influence increased as Spanish colonialism brought increasing wealth to Spain and Spanish influence throughout the New World as well as the Old; the Spanish, along with German mercenaries, even sacked Rome on May 6, 1527, and took Pope Clement VII prisoner in order to bring the Church to heel. Clement finally gave in to Spanish pressure, but never ceased to resent it. For the next eighty years, Spanish influence was a constant factor in most of Italy, particularly the Papal States, and Spanish support could make or break a Pope's reign. At a time when flexibility was most sorely needed in Catholicism, Spanish rigidity pulled the Church sharply to the right, alienating a good portion of Europe, exacerbating an already fraught societal atmosphere, and adding to the military and religious power Spain was gathering all over its far-flung empire, a power that Spain was not averse to using whenever such use served Spanish aspirations. While the Austrian Hapsburgs strove to hold the advance of the Sultan's armies at bay in Hungary and the Balkans, the Spanish Hapsburgs continued to add to the social tensions in Europe by encouraging implacability among the Catholic hierarchy, augmenting this with force of arms when confronted with the rising tide of religious reform.

Working at cross-purposes within itself, the Hapsburg family became inextricably caught up in the social foment of Europe, and complicated it by having mutually exclusive policies among its various rulers. Had there been true commonality among the Hapsburgs, the Renaissance could have expanded rapidly and with much less bloodshed or shut down completely, depending upon which side of the family prevailed. As it was, most of Europe was pulled from pillar to post as the Hapsburgs' power, wealth, and influence shifted, waxed, and waned for the next two centuries. Even those countries not directly involved with Hapsburg interests still had to consider both the Spanish and the Austrian Empires, for the two branches of the family impacted every kingdom, principality, duchy, and republic, from Russia and Scandinavia to North Africa and the New World.

5

MEANWHILE,
IN THE REST OF THE WORLD

OTH 1570 AND 1571 were eventful years, not entirely over-shadowed by the increasing conflict between western Europe and the Ottoman Empire. There were any number of military and political hot spots around the world; discoveries were being made, and other countries, cultures, and continents had problems of their own to deal with, some of which were wholly unaffected by—or even unaware of—the conflict between Europe and the Ottoman Empire.

While the Sultan was declaring war on Venice in 1570, Czar Ivan, called the Terrible or Awe-Inspiring, was scourging the city of Great Novgorod, subjecting its inhabitants to the full range and weight of his wrath. Ivan was a brilliant, powerful, paranoid man with more than sufficient enemies to keep him occupied, but he often discovered (or imagined) rebellions in important centers, and Great Novgorod was a rich trading city with contacts beyond Russia, therefore deserving of the czar's suspicions, at least so far as Ivan was concerned. The destruction was so complete and ruthless that no building was left intact or unplundered, and all foodstuffs but grain were taken, ostensibly to feed Ivan's army, but also to starve the population. All goods and livestock were seized; more than half the population of Great Novgorod was massacred in large groups and thrown into common graves; those who survived were required not to rebuild anything for six weeks—and in a Russian winter, six weeks in the open is as deadly as bullets.

In Nagasaki, Japan, the mayor of the city opened the port to foreigners, ushering in the first real exchange of goods with the West in
all of Japan's history. Merchandise carried on Spanish ships went
from Spain to Mexico, across Mexico by wagon train, then was carried across the Pacific from Acapulco; Japanese trade goods made the
journey in reverse. This was fairly arduous, but it avoided going
around the end of South America or Africa as a means to reach the
Far East, and in fact was a bit faster and much safer than rounding either the Horn or the Cape of Good Hope. There was also a land
crossing along the Isthmus of Panama, which was shorter than the
Mexican crossing, but riskier due to the climate and the Anopheline
mosquito; yellow fever killed more merchants and explorers than European bandits and the native peoples did.

Five North American tribes founded a confederation called the
Iroquois: the Cayuga, Oneida, Seneca, Onondaga, and Mohawk established a council of delegates and a charter that would find echoes
two centuries later in the United States Constitution. And in the
central eastern coast region of North America, native tribesmen
killed a Spanish contingent of soldiers and Jesuits, and as a result of
their losses, the Spanish abandoned plans to colonize farther north
on the east coast than Florida.

Brazilian slave traders on the return trip to Africa and Europe carried sweet potatoes, maize, cassava, and peanuts, all of which served
to augment the African diet as well as that of the sailors making the
crossing. Later these foods would be planted throughout the warmer
parts of Europe, and eventually the slave ships would bring chocolate
to the Old World. Ironically, this improvement of the African diet
led to a population upsurge during the sixteenth and seventeenth
centuries, which contributed to continuing the slave trade with the
Americas.

Bohemian paper-makers became much more important as the need
for quality paper for the burgeoning publishing industry increased. In

Prague, a high-rag-content paper developed that proved to be a superior paper for holding ink evenly and for resisting fading over time. Demand for this paper grew throughout the last third of the century.

One of the first versions of a department store in the world opened in London, the Royal Exchange, which provided selling space to retail merchants, establishing a model upon which many other such mercantile businesses would be based. Abandoning the traditional market square for an enclosed and compartmentalized building, the London Exchange was an immediate hit with middle- and upper-class Londoners, and a new style of shopping for fabric and household goods began to emerge.

William Shakespeare turned six years old in 1570.

In 1571, as if in return to Czar Ivan for the destruction of Great Novgorod, Tartars from Crimea sacked Moscow, putting most of the largely wooden city to the torch and making off with goods, women, and horses. The Russians, having invented prefabricated housing, as the Venetians had invented prefabricated ship assembly, rebuilt almost all of their city in less than three months.

A new Chinese waterwheel improved irrigation in the northern part of the country, and helped in the expansion of the canal system, which, when reversed, provided a degree of flood control that winter. The Chinese began to build drainage ditches and waterwheels for all canals as well as low-lying fields, not only to water the fields, but to promote drainage where needed. Political instability and military incursion stopped the spread of this new engineering within a decade.

The official beginning of European colonization in the Philippines occurred in May, 1571, when Miguel Lopez de Legazpe founded Manila after conquering the native people and moving from the old capital of Cebu to a site more conducive to seagoing traders and ships.

In South America, the first of three planned voyages to map the Amazon River for the Spanish Empire and the Portuguese began, a group of six boats traveling upriver during the low-water season. Among the nineteen Europeans were four missionaries, a Flemish cartographer, six soldiers, and a handful of men looking for treasure. They were gone more than fifteen months; only seven of them actually returned, and of the seven, two died before the year was out.

Dutch clock-makers finally worked out a design for a pocket watch that was sturdy enough to be carried and not too heavy to be held in a standard coat pocket. These pocket watches were very expensive and not terribly reliable timekeepers, but within a decade they had become *the* fashion accessory for the successful businessman.

In Denmark, Tycho Brahe, the innovative astronomer, continued his studies of the heavens; in the following year, he recorded his sightings of a new star that finally demonstrated that Aristotle was wrong in assuming no changes can occur in the outer regions of the sky.

6

GETTING PERSONAL

AS THE OTTOMAN Empire extended its range of marine predation to include those returning from the New World with
treasure, striking from ports in Morocco, Algiers, and other south-
western Mediterranean ports in Islamic hands, the dangers of the
Ottoman-dominated southern and eastern Mediterranean finally
became apparent to all Europe and the might of the Hapsburg Empires was brought into the fight, gradually engaging most of Roman
Catholic Europe in the conflict. After the declaration of war between
Venice and the Ottoman Empire over Cyprus, the ongoing alterca-
tions among the European powers were temporarily set aside so that
a more or less united effort could be mounted to drive the Ottoman
navy from the sea.

The last crucial addition to the mix was an energetic—not to say
fanatical—new pope, Pius V, who fired up religious fervor in support
of the European powers, and in so doing gained—after sustained
effort—the wholehearted support of Spain. Felipe II went so far as to
order his Sicilian fleet, which until this point had been ordered to
avoid assisting other Christian ships against Ottoman foes, to join in
with other European forces in repelling the Turks. The foundation
for the return of the Holy League was laid, embracing Spain and all
the European Spanish territories, including Majorca, Minorca, the
Two Sicilies (Naples, southern Italy, and the island itself), Franche-
Comté in central-eastern France, the Piedmont to the southeast of

France, Sardinia, most of what is now Belgium and the Netherlands; the eastern Hapsburg Empire based at Vienna in Austria and including German, Czech, and Hungarian territory. In addition to this formidable union were the Papal States in Italy; the Spanish client states of Genoa and Corsica, and the ports that were controlled by Genoa; and the Republic of Venice.

France, hemmed in by Hapsburg territories, had to pursue a very delicate balancing act, providing assistance to the Church without increasing Hapsburg claims on French territory, a very real threat. The French king, mindful of the difficulties suffered by François I, was reluctant to do anything that would increase any Hapsburg claim on France, either through past marriages or present treaties. Having no wish to see France become an ancillary part of the Holy Roman Empire or, worse, a puppet of Spain, the king had to walk a fine line that would not completely affront the Church but would not encourage any Hapsburg to assume that France was unable to sustain its autonomy. Although privately encouraging naval officers to help in the fight against the Turks, the King of France—the twenty-one-year-old Charles IX—officially remained strictly neutral.

This unlikely European group entered into a rickety alliance, goaded and pressured by the Pope, who sent out an urgent summons to Catholics everywhere to support this stand against the expansion of Islam. Catholic volunteers came from as far away as Britain and Scandinavia to support the efforts of the Holy League against the Muslim Turks, and for one of the few times in the post-medieval society of the sixteenth century, Europe managed to agree upon the necessity of addressing a common threat.

The Ottoman capture of Cyprus—a longtime Venetian island in Greek waters, and a prize for Europeans and Turks alike—provided an impetus and a focus for European fury, for upon the fall of the fortress city of Famagusta, the Ottoman forces under Lala Mustapha, acting against the terms of surrender of the city, humiliated the revered Venetian commander, Marcantonio Bragadin, and abrogated the terms of the truce they had just concluded, sacking the city, plundering the houses and businesses there, and taking its inhabitants captive to sell as slaves to faithful Ottoman slave merchants.

The Ottoman victors then publicly flayed Bragadin alive and had his skin stuffed with straw, which Lala Mustapha sent back to Turkey to be further degraded in a number of public displays, a deliberately provocative act that Venice could not and would not tolerate, let alone ignore, as this was as direct a challenge to the Venetian presence in the Greek Islands as had ever been issued. For the first time there was sufficient outrage in Europe that efforts were made to assist the Venetians against the Ottomans.

As is obvious, the Hapsburgs were crucial to the struggles against the Ottoman Empire—the eastern and western Hapsburg Empires controlled almost seventy percent of the wealth of Europe, and directly or indirectly ruled over the fortunes of two-thirds of its inhabitants, and had connections, through treaties and marriages with every major royal House in Europe. In the long history of the House of Hapsburg, its influence was at its greatest in the sixteenth and seventeenth centuries, and was never more crucial than at this juncture in European/Ottoman affairs.

With war looming, the Hapsburg rulers gained increasing importance in the conduct of hostilities. In the western Empire, the Spanish King Felipe II was a dour, industrious man with the soul of a bureaucrat and the mind-set of an avid prosecutor; small, brusque, ugly, singleminded, and ferociously dedicated, he actively supported the Spanish Inquisition and mercilessly put down any hints of Protestantism or other heresies that emerged in his territories, although such religious rebellion was rife throughout the rest of Europe, and more tolerated elsewhere than in Spain. He took it as a point of pride that no hint of apostasy was put up with in his realm, and was willing to impose stringent laws to enforce his policy. Felipe

II's reactionary methods justified the kinds of extreme measures the Spanish Inquisition embraced; it is hardly surprising to realize that the Spanish Inquisition reached the apex of its political power during Felipe's reign, with the full might of the government to support it. As Felipe told the Pope, he would rather lose his throne than rule over a kingdom where heresy existed. Such draconian and unremitting persecution of religious and intellectual dissidents marked his governance from beginning to end and complicated his relationships with other European powers where a more accommodating view of religion was emerging.

There was an odd kick in the psychological gallop of the Hapsburgs, the Spanish branch in particular: Felipe II's grandmother was Juana la Loca (Crazy Joan) and she was very well named; she was given to profane outbursts, outrageous behavior of a sexual nature, and she was reputed to have sometimes slept with the embalmed corpse of her dead husband, whom she adored and whom she suspected of continuing his notorious adulteries in death as he had in life. Juana's mother was Isabella the Catholic—the same woman who sponsored Columbus' voyages—who made it her life's work to drive the Jews and the Moors from Spain. It is possible that some of Felipe's fanatical character came from these two women, for he was definitely the obsessive-compulsive type, fond of hierarchical structures, the dogmatic observance of the minutiae of religion, and the fine points of bureaucracy.

His father, the Holy Roman Emperor Charles V, was a very different sort of man—worldly, genial, uncomplicated, secular, generally open-minded, and far more willing to allow his subjects to sort out their religious convictions for themselves—he seems to have been fonder of his bastard daughter, Margaret of Parma, by Johanna van der Gheest, than he was of his legitimate son, Felipe II of Spain, by his empress, Isabella, for he kept her with him as his companion for many years, and made her the unofficial hostess of his court, while

Felipe was sent off to Spain as soon as it was diplomatically possible.

Charles V had other bastards, of course, and supported half a dozen of them at arm's length. His relationship with Margaret was unlike any other he had with his children, legitimate or illegitimate. It may have been because Margaret resembled her father physically and emotionally that he chose to keep her close to him, but it may be that he felt the actual presence of one of the royal family, Felipe, was necessary to preserve Spain. Whatever his reason, Margaret was loyal to her father and upheld his policies when she finally became regent in Flanders, where she supported the Dutch Protestants as much as she could without openly breaking with the Church, or with her half-brother Felipe.

Charles was less inclined to promote his bastard sons, one of whom bears directly on Lepanto: Don Juan of Austria whose mother, Barbara Blomberg, had been a kind of payoff to Charles for aiding a nobleman's widow in her time of need; offering her lovely daughter to the emperor in exchange for a pension seemed a reasonable bargain to all concerned. Barbara's son, Don Juan, became the commander-in-chief of all the ships of the Holy League.

In 1556, worn out and eager to be shut of the ponderous responsibility of the Hapsburg Empire, Charles V retired to the monastery at San Yuste, where the politicking continued in the entrenched rivalry of the Hieronymite Order, which was out of favor with Rome, and the newly founded Society of Jesus (the Jesuits). This ended in the Hieronymite Order being disbanded by Papal Order, and the subsequent rise to power by the Jesuits. By the time of Charles' death in the autumn of 1558, the various factions had engaged the entire Church in their competition, and effectively interrupted the formation of a European front to deal with Ottoman expansion.

Don Juan was raised in Spain by Francisco Massi and his wife Ana under the name of Geronimo, perhaps a subtle sign of support for the ousted Hieronymites (Geronimo and Hieronymus are forms of

Jerome) or to honor Saint Jerome, an early Christian hermit-saint who withdrew from the world to lead the religious life in a cave. Don Juan's foster parents were granted fifty ducats—a handsome sum, the approximate buying-power equivalent of $49,000 in 2005 dollars— per year for his maintenance, and were supervised by Charles' old friend and right-hand man, Luis Quixada, who was Don Juan's only direct link to his father, and whose job it was to keep Don Juan from causing his father any embarrassment.

Geronimo was a handsome child, charming, fair, gregarious, and quick, according to the remaining accounts, and showing early signs of the ability to manipulate people and make them like it—a useful skill for a Hapsburg to have. He passed a favored but isolated childhood in the Spanish countryside. Don Juan remained with the Massis until he was eight, when he was sent to Villagarcia, owned by Quixada's wife, Magdalena de Ulloa. It was hoped that he would learn how to be a courtier instead of a semi-educated villager, and that such instruction would make it possible to find a place in the world that would be appropriate to him as an emperor's bastard. Magdalena was not as easily won over as the villagers of his childhood had been, but he shared her passion for reading, and entered into her enthusiasm for tales of valor. Under her tutelage, he soon became devoutly religious and a great fan of romantic fiction about chivalry and derring-do.

The emperor still didn't know quite what to do with Don Juan, although he thought perhaps a religious life would be best for the boy— and least likely to expose Charles to malign gossip resulting from his son's actions; many nobles enrolled their so-called irregular children in the Church where they could be useful without bringing unwanted attention to various peccadillos. No one bothered to ask Don Juan how he felt about these plans, although Luis Quixada, who knew Don Juan as well as anyone, did his best to convince Charles that Don Juan was more suited for a military life than a monastic one.

At last, in a move to postpone a final decision, Don Juan was sent to the court of his half-brother, Felipe II of Spain, to be a courtier and a possible companion for the troubled Infante, Carlos de Asturias—Don Juan's half-nephew—where he met the son of Charles V's illegitimate daughter, the capable and willful Margaret of Parma, Alessandro Farnese, another half-nephew.

Small, dark, intelligent, and loyal, Alessandro quickly recognized his shared bond with Don Juan, and the two outcasts from Charles V's court found themselves allies in Spain; they were sent to university together and remained devoted friends for all Don Juan's short, hectic life. It was Alessandro Farnese who openly encouraged Don Juan in his desire for a martial life, and who covered for him when he needed someone to run interference for him, such as when Don Juan attempted to sneak off and join the navy, but came down with a fever while traveling to the coast, and so failed in his goal. Still, the escapade finally gave Charles V to think, and he decided that Don Juan probably would not succeed at religious life. He could not then foresee how providential a decision this was.

Don Juan was not particularly welcome at the Spanish court. He was rarely invited to formal or official occasions, could not sit under the Royal Canopy at Mass, and was usually excluded from diplomatic events. Seen as undesirable reminders of Charles' philandering, Don Juan and Alessandro were usually shunted off to the side at state funerals and weddings, and were accorded the least worthy accommodations on those rare occasions when they were summoned to court—this in spite of the ongoing attempts to make Don Juan a model for the Infante, who had come under the scrutiny of the Church for his sporadic support of the Flemish Protestants and the Spanish Moriscos.

Don Carlos remains something of a mystery even now, as he was in life: he was said to be capricious and autocratic, given to bouts of depression, not too bright, and wilful. But the Venetian ambassador said that Carlos was intelligent, well-informed, and capable, subjected to constant thwarting and criticism by his father; the Papal ambassador declared that the Infante bordered on being an unrepentant heretic for his vocal support of the Dutch, and his open disrespect for the Inquisition. Whether young Carlos had any strong convictions about these causes is uncertain—he may have only wanted to annoy his father—but he paid for his recklessness: the Church began an official Inquisitorial Process against him, during which time he was found unaccountably dead in his cell. The usual viewing of the corpse was forbidden by the Church for reasons that make little sense; before interment his body was covered in lye, and he was buried in an obscure grave. Reviewing the various remarks made about him, and a few unbiased accounts of his behavior, it is fairly safe to guess that he had bipolar symptoms, which made him hard to handle and more difficult to influence. In any event, Don Juan had not been able to influence or modify his half-nephew's behavior, which provided Felipe another excuse to slight him.

Crucial to the mix that made Lepanto possible was Pope Pius V, born Antonio Ghislieri in 1504. He began life as a shepherd; his family was impoverished and he had little to look forward to in the outside world except unrelenting labor and abject poverty, so at fourteen he entered the Dominican Order, taking the name Michele. He became a Dominican priest in 1528 and began his long climb to the papacy, serving as Inquisitor for Bergamo and Como. So zealous was he that he caught the attention of Cardinal Gian Pietro Carafa—later Pope Paul IV—who saw him promoted to the Roman Inquisition in 1551. Upon Cardinal Carafa's election as pope, Ghislieri—now calling himself Alessandrino—was appointed Bishop of Nepi and Sutri in 1556, and then Cardinal of Santa Maria sopra Minerva in Rome in 1557.

Elected pope on January 7, 1566, and crowned January 19, Pius began his papacy by banishing feasting and display, and set about instituting a rigorous agenda of austerity. As Bishop of Rome, and the highest political as well as religious authority in Rome, he saw himself as a necessary reformer, restoring the Church to its origins of sacrifice and selflessness. To provide a proper example, he took his meals alone, in the monastic tradition, and abjured all pomp. Described as being "skin and bones" from fasting and similar asceticism, once pope, he continued to wear his monk's habit, and he imposed similar severities on the Church and the citizens of Rome, gaining the grumbling discontent of the Romans and the enthusiastic approval of the Spanish, for whom rigorous and comprehensive nonindulgence was seen as an indication of saintliness and worthy devotion. His policies toward the Protestant states of Europe were far more stringent than his predecessor's had been, which echoed the Spanish demand for an end to all forms of unorthodox Christianity.

Relying heavily on the Inquisition as a tool against heresy, he pursued a policy of no tolerance toward Protestantism, and encouraged all efforts to curtail or stamp out Islam. He surrounded himself with equally rigorous men, and encouraged the promotion of like-minded prelates throughout the Church. As such, he played directly into the hands of the Ottoman Empire, which had been on the brink of civil war for several years, but united against the Roman Catholic forces.

Things were not much better on the Ottoman side: the Sultan at the time was Selim II called "The Grim," as Selim I had been, the son of a Slavic harem slave, he was light-eyed, blond—he often darkened his beard for grand occasions—ambitious, ruthless, humorless—hence his sobriquet—and, according to what has been said about him, although a devout Muslim, an alcoholic. Whether it was wine or depression that accounted for his demeanor, he was viewed as a difficult man and a dangerously aleatory one. His supporters were wary of him, and his enemies despised him with an intensity unusual in the close-knit ruling class. Some of his officers called him Selim the Sot, and claimed his interest in Romania and Hungary was not so much for the glory of Islam or the might of his empire as the acquisition of fine vineyards.

Growing up in the difficult and competitive world of the royal family, Selim rapidly learned to distrust everyone but his mother, and to be careful of his siblings, all of whom were as ambitious as he, and as ready to eliminate him as he was to be rid of them. He was given to melancholy and pessimism, and his temper was considered prodigious even among the Ottoman nobles, which is saying a lot; his outbursts of fury were dreaded by everyone who had any association with him. He had a carnassial hatred of Europeans in general and European merchants in particular, for he saw them—not entirely incorrectly—as degenerate and corrupting the Ottoman way of life, as a challenge to the faith of Islam, and as an evil that was no longer necessary for Ottomans to tolerate; because of this enmity, he unofficially encouraged the kind of excesses that led to the flaying of Marcantonio Bragadin. He gave the corsairs free rein and reaped the rewards of their depredations in the form of tribute and the chance to avail himself of their naval expertise.

The Ottoman navy had some superior talent to draw upon for its ships. Not only did the great corsairs, such as Kara Hodja and Uchiali, participate in naval warfare, but high-ranking military men, including the already-mentioned Lala Mustapha, who had been the tutor of the Sultan Suleiman's children and the Sultan's personal spy before becoming a military commander; Mehmed Suluk, and Mahomet Sirocco, who were just as often skilled in seamanship as land-based fighting, and were expected to excel at both. Although the rivalry among these various captains and commanders was intense, Selim the Grim put them to good use, and was as pleased as it was possible for him to be at the general increase in European maritime losses. As the Ottomans grew increasingly aggressive, European resistance became more unified, justifying Selim's determination—at least to himself—that he was engaged on a righteous course. That both Muslims and Christians misread one another's motives is hardly surprising, given their various religious paradigms and their largely incompatible world views.

Mahomet Sokolli, Selim's son-in-law and grand vizier (roughly equivalent to prime minister), was a capable, clever, crafty fellow, the son of a Bosnian Orthodox priest who had been swept up in the forced Turkish four-times-annually draft when he was a youngster and had grown up in the Turkish army and, later, the court. He had great diplomatic skills, and was sincerely devoted to the Sultan, and maintained his position in the diet (privy council) for almost two decades. It was he who had tipped the balance of power in favor of Selim after the death of Suleiman when war had erupted between Selim and his brother, the forceful and charismatic Bayezid. It was Sokolli who had arranged with the Persian Shah Tahmasp for the return of Bayezid and his sons from Persia, a move that resulted in Bayezid's murder.

For that service and in recognition of his acumen, Selim relied heavily on Sokolli's expertise and allowed him a degree of leeway he did not permit others of his court to have. Sokolli remained a steadfast supporter of the Sultan, dealing with Europeans more successfully than most of the members of the Sultan's court, showing a willingness to bargain when necessary and to bully when possible. He was grudgingly trusted by the Venetians, which trust he used judiciously for many years.

If relying on a non-Turk as grand vizier seems odd, it was, in fact, the most usual arrangement. From the mid-1400s to 1623, only five of forty-eight grand viziers were native-born Turks. Turkish officials had family alliances and ambitions that could work at cross-purposes to the Sultan, but foreign-born grand viziers had no such claims upon their loyalty. Most of the other grand viziers came originally from Christian countries and had been either imperial pages or Janissaries in their youth, taken in the Ottoman quarterly drafting of young men in conquered and client countries.

Another of the prominent non-Turkish naval leaders of the Ottoman Empire was Uchiali (also sometimes called el Louck Ali,

Ochiali, Uchali, etc.). Born and raised as a fisherman in Calabria, he was kidnapped by Ali Ahmed while still a youth and chained to an oar in an Algerian galliot. His conversion to Islam as a means of exacting revenge on a Muslim shipmate seems typical of his character as it is known to history. Muslim oarsmen were not slaves as such, since technically no Muslim can own another, and by converting, Uchiali gained the right to defend his honor, which he did by killing the oarsman who had offered him an intolerable insult. No one openly questioned his conversion—which was very convenient for Uchiali—yet Uchiali was touchy about it for almost a decade after it occurred, and had been known to beat men senseless for doubting the sincerity of his belief.

The single-combat defeat of the man who insulted him brought Uchiali to the attention of Dragut, the slave-capturing corsair, who made Uchiali his lieutenant, for as a Calabrese fisherman, Uchiali knew the southern coast of Italy well, and could guide Dragut's ships on raids. His devotion to Dragut was intense, and through his loyalty and cunning, Uchiali eventually, in 1568, became the Ottoman governor of Algiers. As his successes grew, so did his ambition; all through his rise to power and influence Uchiali was always on the lookout for a chance to achieve further victories.

During the Morisco Revolt in Spain, Uchiali, perceiving that it was unlikely that the Moriscos would prevail, was unwilling to assist the revolt, limiting the arms he provided to what the men of Algiers were willing to donate. The rumor at the time was that the Spanish had bribed him handsomely to keep out of the Morisco Revolt, enabling Uchiali to line his pockets without risking defeat that would certainly have damaged his reputation.

The diplomatic relations of the Ottoman Empire and Europe continued to erode as Ottoman military expansion increased, and gradually a confrontation was understood to be inevitable. Both sides began to prepare for what was undoubtedly to come. But the European factions still were at each other's throats almost as much as they were at the Turks'. It took all the determination of the Pope to cobble together the two Hapsburg dynasties and secure the guarded support of France in order to revive what was called the Holy League

By trying to get European cooperation, the Pope had to make terms with various European states, even those with Protestant populations, which was not the kind of situation that made for cordial international relations. It was a precarious time politically, in large part because there had been pogroms undertaken against many religious groups in Europe, and resentment as well as resistance was building. Given this religious turmoil, Europe took longer to respond to the crisis in the Mediterranean than might have been the case a hundred years earlier, or a hundred years later.

Policies aimed at achieving a better balance between Protestants and Catholics had not yet taken hold, and there had been religious bloodshed in many parts of Europe which hampered the forming of the Holy League, for many Protestants feared—and not without cause—that once the Ottomans had been dealt with, Catholic ferocity might be turned on non-Catholic enclaves. Certain of the Protestant leaders, while wanting to defend Christianity, were disinclined to assist Pius V. The Pope, being rigorously orthodox, found these negotiations particularly trying. Even once the basic terms of the alliance had been established, the difficulties continued, not only on religious grounds, but through the intense rivalry of various military leaders, each championed—and occasionally egged on—by the various rulers involved, most of whom jealously guarded their sovereignty and prestige. Most significant was the rivalry of the various European admirals brought into the Holy League to participate in the effort to drive the Ottomans from the Mediterranean.

Possibly the most intense rivalry was the ongoing one of Genoese and Venetians; Genoa had suffered a crushing defeat at Venetian hands on January 1, 1380, and during the two intervening centuries had never got over the humiliation, in large part because the Venetians never let them forget it. Both great maritime states claimed leadership and superiority in naval expertise, which dragged other allies into the debate, and put egos as well as battles on the line. The long tradition of maritime rivalry made the establishment of a chain of command within the forces of the Holy League especially tricky, and it took all the prestige the Pope could muster to keep the ongoing bickering among the various high-ranking leaders from fracturing the alliance beyond all possibility of repair.

After the Venetians refused to hand over Cyprus, a sizable portion of the Ottoman navy was dispatched in a show of force to the eastern Mediterranean, the Adriatic, and the Aegean Seas, where there were reports of seeing the formidable array of ships all through the late spring and early summer of 1570. Although only minor skirmishes were fought, it was apparent that when the Venetians threw down the glove, the Ottomans had picked it up, confident that the Europeans could not maintain any concerted effort against them. These decisions on both sides led to an escalation of hostilities that proved much easier to incite than to contain.

Arriving at Rhodes in June, the Turkish fleet prepared for the next stage of the campaign. Thanks to Sokolli's clever manipulations, which were aided and abetted by Lala Mustapha and the Sultan's other son-in-law, Piale Pasha, who had disgraced himself so utterly at the Siege of Malta and then brought suspicion upon himself through his unseemly profiting from the assault he ordered on the Genoese enclave on Chios, a Greek island near Smyrna. This way, if anything went wrong at Cyprus, Sokolli would have scapegoats in plenty on whom to fix blame for the failure of the venture, just as he could claim that his plans had not been accurately carried out. At the same time, he could also claim credit for the success of the campaign if the Ottoman forces triumphed.

In July of 1570, on Sokolli's command, and with the full support of the navy and corsairs, a very large force of Ottoman fighters landed on Cyprus at Limassol: fifty thousand regular troops, and two thousand five hundred crack cavalry, along with an uncounted number of conscripted young men from client countries; they were well-armed, reasonably well-trained, and spoiling for a fight. Meeting with only token resistance, they advanced rapidly to Nicosia, the capital of Cyprus, where the Venetians were concentrated in an ancient fortress, preparing for what they had been told would be a short-lived siege. The Venetian governor, Nicolo Dandolo, was determined to resolve the problem diplomatically, and so had not bothered to provision either the city or the fortress for a long siege—a decision that would lead to disaster for the Venetians.

7

OPENING GAMBITS

W HILE THE OTTOMAN Empire was in the process of occupying Cyprus, the Venetians and Spain were involved in
diplomatic negotiations with the Pope, under the immediate auspices
of Pius' nephew, Cardinal Alessandrino, trying to forge an alliance that
would suit all the parties concerned, a mission that seemed doomed
from the start. Spain, represented by the Archbishop of Burgos, Cardinal Granvelle, and Don Juan de Zuniga, was determined not to let the
Venetians take advantage of this cooperative effort and wrest command of the troops away from a Spanish-approved commander. Felipe
II did not want to have to defend Venetian claims throughout the
Adriatic and the Mediterranean, and for that reason, pushed for
Genoese control of the ships intended to seek out and destroy the Ot-
toman galleys; Genoa was firmly under Spanish control and would put
Spanish interests ahead of all others', including the Pope's.

The Most Serene Republic of Venice was represented by Michele
Surian, the ambassador to Rome. Venice was pushing for an immediate response to the Ottoman invasion of Cyprus, arguing that other
islands would soon be invaded if nothing was done to throw the
Turks off Cyprus, while Spain attempted to keep the Venetian interests from dictating the nature of the alliance, for it was not in Spain's
interest to promote an across-the-board war with the Ottoman Empire. At the same time, both sides knew that such Turkish expansion
as the invasion of Cyprus could not be ignored. Driven by force of

circumstance, the Europeans set up a kind of experimental expedition to see if a Holy League venture could be made viable.

As a result of these arrangements, forty-nine war galleys of the Sicilian flotilla, under the command of the King of Spain's personal appointee, thirty-one-year-old Genoese Admiral Giannandrea Doria, rendezvoused with fourteen Venetian war galleys, flying the banner not of Venice, but of the Papal States, on August 20, 1570, at Otranto on the southeastern shore of Italy. Together, they headed for Crete and the main body of Venetian war galleys. Arriving eleven days later, they were met by fifty-four war galleys under the Venetian Admiral Hieronimo Zanne.

The leader of this diverse group was appointed by the Pope, the Roman nobleman Marcantonio Colonna, who was a capable diplomat—which he needed to be, for the Genoese and the Venetians had been bickering steadily since leaving Otranto, and continued their sniping even as they prepared to hunt out the Ottomans, which brought an edginess to morale for all the Europeans involved, much to Colonna's dismay.

The Colonne were an ancient Roman family whose roots, like the Orsini, the della Roverei, and the Fabiani, went back to Republican Rome, and as such had ties to many of the noble families in Europe, as well as centuries and centuries of working inside the Italian Establishment, however it was defined at any given time. The awkward side of his command was that both Zanne and Doria were vastly more experienced seamen than Colonna, and touchy as tomcats about their skills and status, and therefore disinclined to take orders from a Roman politician, no matter how well-connected he was. This resentment, in turn, required that Colonna redouble his diplomatic efforts in order to maintain an acceptable level of camaraderie among the Genoese and the Venetians as they began their mission; capable as Colonna was at handling awkward situations, this one pressed his skills to their limits. During their voyage, matters did not improve.

Giannandrea Doria proved to be a reluctant warrior, even though—or perhaps because—he had a good deal of experience fighting the Ottoman forces at sea, experiences that had left him cautious, stubborn, determined, and unwilling to take chances. He was proud to the point of vanity, and had a high opinion of his own reputation that he believed made him the maritime superior to all others involved in the hunt. He was also worried about the potential for treachery and disaster, which he perceived as intended to destroy his reputation. The reason for this intense and highly personalized circumspection may also have been due to the fact that a dozen of the Sicilian galleys participating in this campaign were his own personal property, and so he was disinclined to risk losing the ships and the lease-money they commanded from the Spanish crown. Doria's profiting from renting out his warships was nothing new—almost all high-ranking military mariners owned war galleys and profited from their leased use in battle.

Doria and Zanne, dissatisfied from the first, became increasingly critical and competitive; it took all of Colonna's considerable talents as a negotiator to keep the Genoese and Venetians working in concert as they gathered at Candia, Crete, where more prestige was at risk. It began to look as if a unified assault by European forces would be impossible.

In all, there were 205 ships assembled, including supply and scout ships as well as war galleys. While not an overwhelming number, there were ships and men sufficient to demand at least an equal number of Turks to contain them. Unluckily for the Christian force, not far from Cyprus the Ottoman ships, under Piale Pasha, were a larger number of warships and supply vessels, and they were generally better armed. Giannandrea Doria was unwilling to undertake an assault against the Ottoman fleet, although Marcantonio Colonna was prepared to go forward. Some of the European officers began to suspect that Doria would not fight at all, whether out of greed and thus a

minimization of the risk to his galleys; out of loyalty to the King of
Spain, whose man Doria so clearly was; or out of a loss of nerve from
his defeat in the earlier Tripoli attacks, no one knew. In any case, for
many of the European forces, Doria's obstinacy struck a sour note,
and led to a degree of rancor among the various ships' captains, many
of whom were itching to have at the Ottomans.

Doria himself insisted that half the war galleys were not in fighting
condition, with insufficient oarsmen to match the corsairs' ships, and
would in all likelihood be lost almost as soon as any real battle began.
He claimed they were inadequately provisioned for a lengthy campaign, and that without a much better arrangement for resupply, the
project was doomed to failure. There were some indications that this
might be an accurate assessment: neither Venice nor Genoa had sent
their best war galleys to this force, and an outbreak of fever had reduced the number of fit, working oarsmen by almost twenty percent.
Still, Doria's posture of dogmatic nonengagement left most of the
participants feeling frustrated and insulted, which added to the internal strife Colonna had to contend with.

The Venetians, growing more pugnacious as the Genoese dragged
their metaphorical heels, argued that since more than half their oarsmen were Christians, either volunteering or being paid to row, they
would prove the match for the Ottoman crews, which were largely
made up of slaves. The bickering continued for more than two weeks,
while Colonna, aware that there was some validity in all arguments,
tried to make up his mind before the weather changed, and almost all
ships forced to head for safe harbors. At last Doria conceded that
something had to be undertaken, provided it was not too hazardous. So on September 17, 1570, the ships set out to attack Piale
Pasha's base on Rhodes. This goal was a compromise, and most of the
15,800 men on the European ships knew it.

By September 23, the Europeans learned that Nicosia on Cyprus
had fallen to Lala Mustapha and Ali Pasha, the son of an important

muezzin from one of the Sultan's mosques; this changed the various problems the Europeans faced, and it made the stakes they played for much higher. It was no longer possible for the Europeans to make use of a symbolic victory, such as Rhodes would provide.

So for once Doria and Zanne agreed: challenging the fortifications at Rhodes would not be a sufficient response to the Ottoman treachery breaking their Cyprus treaty entailed, and Rhodes would have little or no impact on Ottoman ambitions. Doria took satisfaction in knowing that Colonna's missed opportunity to stop the Ottoman advance would not reflect badly on him or his sponsor, Felipe II, but would provide him excellent reason to call the shots in the next phase of their campaign, which he—Doria—was already planning. His behavior left no doubt that he expected to take Colonna's place as leader of the Holy League naval forces. In anticipation of his promotion, Doria suggested that the European force return to its various home ports for the purposes of conferring about what to do come the spring, when it would once again be sailing weather.

One of the immediate results of this dramatic change of fortunes brought about the realization that there was no way to continue the alliance with Marcantonio Colonna in charge; another commander would have to be found, and not, it was almost universally acknowledged, Giannandrea Doria, no matter what the Spanish hoped for, for that level of favoritism might be enough to drive the Venetians out of the Holy League, which would be disastrous. Over vigorous Spanish objections, Colonna looked elsewhere for an appropriate commander.

It was understood that the commander chosen would have to be one acceptable enough to all parties to avoid the constant carping and arguing that had marked this trial run of the ships of the Holy League. It was also—not so publicly—decided that newer galleys were needed, with the latest improvements, so that, even if they had to fight a larger Ottoman fleet, as all their intelligence said they would, they would have the most recent improvements to increase the effectiveness of their vessels. There was no question now that there would be at least one major battle ahead in this campaign, and if the Europeans had a hope of winning, they would have to take the winter to make all-out preparations.

The preparations would not be limited to arms, but would include adequate amounts of food and water. Because there was no means to refrigerate food, the preferred foods were beans, oats, peas, lentils, hard tack, cheeses, barrels of salt beef, smoked bacon, *baccala* (dried, salted cod—a Venetian specialty), and crates of live chickens, which would provide eggs until they ended up in the stew pot. The officers fared a little better, having bread and oil added to their diet, and occasionally wine as well, but for the most part, food aboard ship was chosen for lack of spoilage over all other considerations. Providing enough food for as big a fleet as they were about to assemble would take coordination and money as well as a great deal of contrivance.

8

FIRST LULL

DESPITE THE SUCCESS on Cyprus, there was trouble brewing for Lala Mustapha and Ali Pasha. Both men had risen from fairly obscure beginnings, and had not done so by being models of virtue. Ali was by far the more personable of the two, and the one who had the support of many of the Sultan's wives and concubines. The mosque at which he and his father served overlooked the Sultan's scraglio; Ali's strong, beautiful voice was well-known to the Sultan's women, most of whom supported his advancement. Lala Mustapha had tutored the Sultan's children, and while he was a capable instructor, the support this earned him was somewhat less predictable, for his severity had gained him a degree of enmity as well as respect. Both men were pitiless in war, and although they rarely had the opportunity to give free rein to their impulses, Cyprus provided them the occasion to do so.

The capture of Nicosia was particularly recreant; after a forty-six-day siege, the Turks sent an Orthodox monk to ask if the fortress would surrender on terms, which generally meant that the defenders would not be killed. Since there were only about 500 men left manning the fortress, terms were accepted, and the Venetians agreed to surrender with the expectation that the soldiers would be spared, although they would become slaves.

As soon as the treaty was signed, the Ottoman soldiers went on a rampage, killing the Christian soldiers, including the Venetian governor of Cyprus, Nicolo Dandolo, and then cut loose through the city, resulting in the massacre of between 16,000 and 20,000 inhabitants, and the sacking and pillaging of all the houses and businesses left untouched by the siege. Only attractive young men and women were spared from the slaughter, and they were sent to the slave markets in Constantinople. One of the captives of the Turks taken aboard an Ottoman war galley—a young woman according to legend—lit the powder magazine with a candle and blew up the ship with its soldiers, crew, 800 captives, and untold plunder.

Once Nicosia fell, the last remaining site of resistance on Cyprus was the Crusader fort of Famagusta, and Lala Mustapha dispatched his cavalry there, carrying the heads of Venetian dignitaries and military officers on their lances and saddles not only as trophies but as an encouragement to the garrison to surrender. Judging from the response of the defenders of Famagusta, this tactic had the opposite effect to what was intended, for the Venetians took the severed heads as an indication that they would receive no mercy from the Ottoman forces, and prepared to defend Famagusta to the last man.

On September 1, 1570, Lala Mustapha set up his first siege guns. It was the wrong time of year to mount a successful siege since most of the naval fleet had been sent off to winter ports, leaving only a token blockade of forty war galleys at Cyprus, and Mustapha was therefore lacking in ships to hold on to the island, a situation that the Venetians did their best to use advantageously. The Ottoman siege was breached at least once in January by Venetian Marcantonio Quirini, coming in from Crete with sixteen galleys and three supply ships; he rescued civilians and wounded from Famagusta, provided gunpowder and munitions to the defenders, as well as food and about 1,500 soldiers, and did much to bolster esprit de corps for the Europeans.

Upon learning of this—and the news was carried as quickly as scout ships could travel—the Sultan was outraged. Son-in-law or no son-in-law, Piale Pasha was held accountable for the failure to take all of Cyprus before winter. Using fast-sailing scout ships to carry his orders, the Sultan relieved Piale Pasha of duty in disgrace sixteen days later, and summoned him back to Constantinople, where it was hoped he could do no more harm, and where Sokolli, his former rival, could keep an eye on him. This left the Cyprus campaign in the ruthless hands of Lala Mustapha.

Taking advantage of the situation, Sokolli sent a clandestine mission to Venice, offering the Venetians a separate peace if they would disassociate themselves from the Papal and Spanish forces. Sokolli held out the possibility of saving the defenders of Famagusta from a similar fate to the population of Nicosia to increase the incentive for a Venetian settlement, a proposal which gained the support of a sizable minority of the Maggior Consiglio.

On the other side of this debate, Pope Pius did his utmost to rally Christians to the cause of their religion. He strove to keep the Venetians and the Spanish sufficiently in accord to maintain a real campaign against the Ottoman navy. He kept up the pressure in spite of doubts expressed by the Spanish and the Venetian representatives about the possibility of prevailing over the Ottoman aggressors. The Pope even persuaded Cosimo dei Medici, the Grand Duke of Tuscany, to sponsor a knightly order for those defending Christians at sea against the Turks.

King Charles IX of France refused to participate, and not only because French ships were not being hunted by corsairs as Genoese, Spanish, and Venetians were, but because the French were seeking to block any more Hapsburg inroads into France. Only the Knights of Malta—the majority of whom were French—supported the idea of a Holy League; more than any other French outpost, they had felt the heavy hand of the Ottoman navy directly. Pope Pius continued to lobby for a Holy League in early 1571, tirelessly pursuing European support from such unlikely sources as Portugal and Poland to help shore up his position with the vacillating Venetians and the recalcitrant Spanish.

The Pope was not the only one making the most of the winter slack-time. Sokolli took full advantage of the four months to entertain the secretary of the Maggior Consiglio, stressing how peace with the Sultan would benefit the Venetians, allowing them to keep and expand their markets and thereby to become the preeminent power in Europe through their association with the Ottoman Empire. Only the certainty that such a bargain would be disastrous to Europe and Christianity—and therefore ruinous to business—made the Maggior Consiglio hesitate to embrace this superficially generous offer. Only the certainty that Venice had greater enemies in Constantinople than they had in Europe kept the Consiglio from making their deal with Sokolli. After all, Piale Pasha had fallen suddenly and completely from power, and that could happen to Sokolli, and then where would Venice be, but caught in an alliance with their enemies and unable to ask for the support of even their weakest friends? There was also the chance, as well, that Sokolli might be making some kind of deal with Pius V, which would leave Venice wholly powerless against a superior foe. Then again, if Venice did accept a treaty with the Ottoman Empire, might not the Pope consider it a betrayal, and put Venice under interdict, or worse?

Finally the Spanish were persuaded to mount and launch a real naval campaign against the Turks late in the summer of 1570, in concert with Venice and the Papal forces. This made the campaign feasible, and the officials of all governments began to hammer out the terms of their affiliation. Working in the storm season when most fleets were in winter harbor and could not be put into action, the military leaders and diplomats labored steadily to come up with acceptable conditions for the campaign. Agreeing on a plunder-split of one for the Pope, two for Venice, and three for Spain, the bargain was struck in March of 1571, after a last spasm of disagreement following Mass on March 7, which saw both Spain and Venice still hedging their bets, with the chance of making a go of the Holy League more remote than before. But the Pope prevailed and the treaty was signed: it was agreed that in perpetuity the three forces would send out 200 galleys and 100 supply ships, carrying 50,000 infantry. In a decision of diplomatic acumen as great as any in his reign, Pope Pius vested command of the Holy League forces in twenty-four-year-old Don Juan of Austria, the bastard son of the late Holy Roman Emperor Charles V, and half-brother of Felipe II of Spain.

This clever move not only gave the young bastard something important to do, it all but guaranteed the help and support of the Austrian branch of the Hapsburg family, including more soldiers and gunpowder for the war galleys as well as access to safe harbors along the Dalmatian coast. Don Juan could not be allowed to be left floundering, and Felipe II's support was lukewarm, requiring the Austrian branch to take up the slack in European support. The pace of planning stepped up.

9

FAMAGUSTA

THE RUGGED OLD Crusaders' fort of Famagusta was well-situated to withstand sieges: the harbor was small and as easy to blockade as it was protective of any merchant ship anchored under its guns. Its garrison was small—7,000 for town and fortress combined—and the town's defenses minimal. Marcantonio Bragadin, the governor, working with Astor Baglione, the military commander, had made the most of what they had. They tore down buildings beyond the relatively inadequate fortifications in order to open up more lines of fire, as well as to garner more building materials with which to build up the ramparts of the town that in many places were no taller than a man, in anticipation of the arrival of the Turks from Nicosia. They also moved over 800 civilians to safety, and accepted another 500 as volunteer defenders; these were mainly Greek Orthodox Christians, who disliked the Catholic Venetians but had come to realize that they would not want to be under Ottoman rule, and therefore had decided to help the Venetians, at least for the present.

By the time the Turks arrived with their grisly collection of heads, they found the defenders of Famagusta well organized and disinclined to be frightened by such gruesome displays—in fact, quite the reverse. This small, determined garrison was prepared to hold their fortifications for as long as possible—that turned out to be slightly more than ten months, buying crucial time for the Holy League to prepare for war.

Making their winter camp on Cape Greca, west of the city, the Turks set up twenty-five guns aimed at the town's low parapets, and proceeded to blast away at them. Famagusta settled down for a long, unhappy winter, which was made more unpleasant by an early and unusually turbulent storm season. The defenders made occasional cavalry raids on the Ottoman camp, and other groups of volunteers made sallies directly at the Turkish cannon, lobbing them with hand-thrown explosives, thereby damaging many of the Ottoman guns. Such risky excursions did fairly little damage in and of themselves, but the cumulative effect was telling.

In one particularly daring move, the Venetians sappers, led by Nestor Martinengo, undermined the Turkish tunnel that had been dug with the intention of breaching the walls. Martinengo and his men, having dug the lower tunnel, made a daring raid on the higher, Turkish tunnel, and carried off the gunpowder meant to bring down the town walls, placed it in their own, deeper tunnel, and collapsed the Turkish tunnel instead. For a time this curtailed Turkish attempts to undermine the Famagusta walls, but inevitably, the tunneling began again, and eventually succeeded, particularly as the defenders ran low on gunpowder and had little to spare to blow up Turkish sappers. This was the kind of bold move that could only work once, and it was a lucky thing for the Venetians that the Martinengo raid succeeded so well, for they would have no second opportunity.

The plight of the Christian defenders at Famagusta was soon known throughout Europe and there was increasing public awareness of the need to mount some kind of relief effort; the implications of another Venetian loss of such an important outpost were borne in upon the Europeans as a bad sign for the future in regard to Turkish ambitions. Finally Christian Europe understood the danger these island-hopping advances represented and, with the concerted efforts of the Pope to keep the ordeal of the Venetian defenders of Fama-gusta in the public eye, began to support the Holy League. Without the siege of Famagusta as a prod, it is unlikely that Pope Pius could have sustained his efforts at bringing the European powers around to his point of view. It is also unlikely that the Venetians would have continued to evade the Turks on the issue of a private treaty had not their own forces been manning Famagusta.

As demanding as the siege was, it had the effect that nothing else had been able to achieve: it suspended the internal hostilities that were rife in Europe and redirected the general attention to the Ottoman advances and the need to contain them while there was still a chance of preparing a successful counter-campaign. Venice, with its far-flung merchant empire, was an anomaly among European states, with a significant number of the people of the city tied to maritime trade and therefore familiar with distant ports; most Europeans had very little concept of the Greek Islands and the ongoing expansion of the Ottoman Empire, except that it was a dangerous force of un-Christian zealots who wanted nothing more than to destroy Europe. Famagusta changed that—at least in regard to where Cyprus was; no matter how remote Cyprus might have seemed to the vast number of Europeans—most of whom never ventured more than thirty miles from home in a lifetime—Famagusta made it real, immediate, and worthy of concern.

Fortunately for the Europeans, the time of year the siege began worked to their advantage: the Turkish winter patrol of the blockaded harbor of Famagusta was maintained by seven galleys, hardly more than a token force, and one that could not withstand any serious attacks by concentrated sea power, a fact that was brought crushingly home at the end of January, 1571, when the Ottoman galleys, anchored in Costanza Bay, or beached there, depending on which report you believe, were surprised by the sudden arrival of sixteen Venetian war galleys escorting three well-armed and deeply laden merchant ships, bringing supplies and food to the defenders of Famagusta. Caught in a very bad situation, the Ottoman galleys did the only sensible thing—they made for open sea, Marcantonio Quirini's brand new, higher-decked war galleys in eager pursuit and causing as much damage to the Ottoman ships as they could without creating an actual confrontation that neither side was actually prepared for. After sinking three of the seven Turkish ships, Quirini abandoned the chase as night came on.

Once the town was resupplied, 1,600 new troops added to the ranks of the defenders, and the wounded, sick, and civilians removed from Famagusta, Quirini's war galleys went on an audacious trip around Cyprus, sinking two Turkish supply ships; carrying off oars, ropes, and sails; raiding Turkish food supplies; burning Turkish watchtowers; attacking small fortifications; and sending landing parties ashore to interfere with Ottoman couriers, patrols, signalmen, and other military communications. A second blockade-runner sent directly from Venice brought an additional 800 troops under Onorio Scotto, who carried a letter of encouragement and praise from the Maggior Consiglio, all of which improved the morale of the Famagusta defenders and annoyed the Turks, just as the Maggior Consiglio intended.

The governor of Venetian-controlled Crete, Sebastian Venier, wanted to send his ninety-seven galleys to help lift the siege at Cyprus, certain that an attack in winter would have the advantage of surprise and would be worth the risks of the bad weather they would be certain to encounter, given what they could gain. Venier had experience fighting Turks: he had defended Corfu against them the previous year, countering the Ottoman attacks on the island of Corfu with widely dispersed cavalry and sallies onto the coast of Albania, then in Ottoman hands. He had more than enough reason to want to attack the Turks, although his available force was small, but his plans were vetoed by his senior military officers, all of whom had heard that there was a major buildup of Ottoman ships at Cyprus that would be sufficient to destroy the Venetian vessels from Crete. Venier, then in his seventies and an attorney by trade, vowed to preserve Venetian Greek islands for Venice.

Feeling encouraged, the European forces began to consider a major attack on Ottoman naval installations, and to work out the means not only to find the main body of the Ottoman fleet, but to prepare strategies for fighting this enormous flotilla. In terms of European propaganda, Famagusta was a triumph and a rallying point. But, of course, like all sieges, it had to end, and with that end came more trouble for both sides.

10

A CHANGE IN FORTUNE

URIOUS AT THE Famagusta standoff, Sultan Selim II declared that there were to be no new military targets undertaken by his naval forces anywhere until Famagusta fell. The Divan agreed, for this advisory council was smarting from the Famagusta siege as much as the Sultan was: a handful of Venetians had managed to halt or delay the campaign that was underway against the Venetian holdings in the Aegean and Adriatic Seas as well as stopping the planned invasion of Italy itself. To bring about the capitulation of the defenders of Famagusta, Selim II ordered most of his war galleys at winter anchorage near the Dardanelles out of port before March—almost a month before such an order would usually be issued—and commanded that the main flotillas of his navy join forces.

Ottoman ships set out from Egypt under Mahomet Sirocco—named for the hot south wind, and to distinguish him from another Mahomet, who led the ships from Negroponte—and from Chios and Rhodes, resulting in a company of two hundred Ottoman ships, all bound to reinforce the Ottoman ships and troops at Cyprus, and goaded on by the demands of the Sultan. The lead ships—approximately seventy in number—under Ali Pasha, the harem's favorite, arrived off Cyprus in April, landing Janissaries and other soldiers in front of the besieged city at Costanza Bay, resulting in between 100,000 and 225,000 Ottoman soldiers on the ground at Famagusta, half of them well-trained and well-armed attack troops, all under the bellicose command of Lala Mustapha, whose pride was damaged by the long siege.

The Venetian defenders of Famagusta, now reduced to roughly 4,000 men, continued to hold off the massed Turks, their grenadiers stopping all Turkish tunneling under their walls, their support teams building up blasted walls and reinforcing gates and rooftops against the battery from Lala Mustapha's seventy-four cannon. The worst of these siege guns were four basilisks—massive guns made of brass that shot 200-pound balls—and they became the target of any and all the defenders could throw at them, from arrows and shot to what their own diminishing supply of ordnance provided for their cannon. In order to be able to make swift responses to any attacks, the Venetian military leaders made shelters up against their walls, a tactic that provided quick receptions to the Turks but also put many of their men at greater risk of injury; over the next month, this made inroads in the number of high-ranking Venetian officers available for duty.

Problems of supply hampered both sides of the conflict: the Venetians were getting low on almost everything, and running the Ottoman blockade to get food, ammunition, and other essentials to them grew more dangerous with every passing day as the Turkish ships kept up steady patrols around the island. Supply problems were not limited to the besieged; the Ottoman forces, by their very numbers, needed a constant stream of men and materiel. That stream provided the Venetians with targets which they took regular advantage of, and slowed down the Ottoman advance by picking off the slaves given the tasks of off-loading supply ships, making the Ottoman offense more difficult in the face of irregular supplies.

Eventually by sheer weight of superior numbers of men and weapons, the Turkish barrage proved to be too much, and the walls were breached at a point near the weapons' stockpile inside Famagusta's walls. The Ottoman attack lasted almost five hours and, against all expectations, the Turks failed to overrun the city. The

Turks managed to open another part of the wall and spent more than six hours attempting to get through, and again they failed, sustaining heavy losses in their efforts. A third attack at all weakened parts of the wall, in early July, also failed, and Lala Mustapha was outraged. He had lost over 50,000 men and had yet to occupy the city—a serious embarrassment for him personally as well as a slap in the face to his crack troops.

But the defenders had paid a high price for the siege: more than half the Venetian troops defending the city were dead, they were running out of gunpowder, they had eaten all their horses and had only a few barrels of flour left. They might be able to hold off one more assault, but that would be the last of it; Famagusta was finished, and Marcantonio Bragadin knew it, for he had received a dispatch from the Maggior Consiglio informing him that they would not send a hundred galleys to raise the siege. Bragadin was advised to treat with Mustapha while he could still have bargaining power that would benefit his men. Bragadin sent a covert message to Mustapha, asking for an opportunity to work out terms for the surrender of Famagusta, which took place on August 1, 1571. For four days its terms held.

11

RENEGING

THE TREATY LALA Mustapha and Marcantonio Bragadin had
signed for the surrender of Famagusta had guaranteed life and
freedom to those living inside the walls: those who wished to remain
and live under Ottoman rule would not be deprived of property,
those who preferred to leave would not be hindered, and could take
all their movable belongings with them. The Venetian soldiers could
keep their personal weapons and would be carried by Turkish galleys
to the Venetian garrison at Crete, along with the sick and wounded;
there would be no claiming of conquerors' rights to abuse the conquered in any way. No church would be looted or its contents destroyed. All in all, reasonable terms for honorable foes; Marcantonio
Bragadin had done well for Famagusta, and for Venice, and everyone
knew it—Ottomans as well as Europeans. It seemed that after their
long ordeal, a satisfactory end had been achieved.

For three days all went according to the terms of Mustapha's and
Bragadin's agreement, and it was increasingly apparent that the truce
would benefit all the survivors of the siege, Turk and Venetian alike.
The Venetians were confident that Bragadin had saved them in ne-
gotiating such a favorable surrender, because the Ottomans were very
righteous about their pledged word, as all of them had reason to
know. Mustapha, acting in the capacity of the Sultan's deputy, was
doubly bound to maintain the terms of the truce, for if he in any way
went against the truce, he compromised not only himself, but the

Sultan. Anything that smirched Selim II's honor usually brought swift and dreadful retribution from the Sultan, so such drastic acts were rarely undertaken. As one of the Venetian survivors reported a few years later: "No one would have thought that the Turks would go back on such an agreement as they had made, not just for the Sultan's sake, but for their Holy Book, which is as sacred to them as the Testaments are to Christians." One of the few survivors later reported that on the third day of the truce, Mustapha had boasted of his high standards of integrity, and his men had echoed his sentiments.

But on the fourth day after the truce had been signed, Lala Mustapha apparently decided to abrogate the conditions of the truce, and in a spectacular disregard of Islamic doctrine and Turkish tradition went back on his sworn word. During his daily meeting with Marcantonio Bragadin, he accused the Venetian of killing Turkish prisoners and plotting to keep the Turkish galleys carrying the defeated Venetians to Crete so that they could be used as Venetian ships. He also charged Bragadin with withholding treasure from the Turkish victors. When Bragadin would not be provoked by any of these insults and slights, Mustapha ordered his escort killed by swordsmen waiting outside his tent, and put Bragadin in chains, then had the Venetians on the Ottoman galleys chained to oars, their promised freedom revoked, and when all this was done, Mustapha ordered Bragadin's deputy hanged, and his body left to rot over the city's ruined gates.

For the next week, as a continuation of his deliberate acts of cruelty, Mustapha had Bragadin's nose and ears cut off, he was pilloried in Famagusta and dragged around the Ottoman camp in nothing but a loincloth and a donkey's saddle, and made to kiss the ground in front of Lala Mustapha's tent. The Ottoman soldiers were encouraged to throw garbage and excrement on him, and to mock his misery, and to pull hairs from his beard—a particularly nasty affront in sixteenth-century Islamic culture. Lala Mustapha himself came out to spit on the Venetian, and to empty his chamber pot over the old man's head. All of these humiliations were meticulously reported by Mustapha's personal scribe to show he had regained his stature as a formidable leader, and the report was sent off to the Divan. Finally, Mustapha had Marcantonio Bragadin flayed alive, his skin stuffed and further subjected to abasements, such as being hanged from the yardarm of Lala Mustapha's ship and depended from the broken walls of Famagusta, before sending the trophies taken from Famagusta and the skin to the Sultan, who eventually had the skin locked in the slaves' prison in a gesture of contempt, a dire insult in Ottoman culture of the time.

While most of these heinous acts were intended to horrify the Venetians as a means of lessening their inclination to make war, they were also geared to undermine any attempt at a negotiated peace with Venice, which Mustapha's most potent rival, Grand Vizier Sokolli, was rumored to be trying to achieve through diplomatic meetings with the Venetian representatives in Constantinople, having engaged the French to assist him. Mustapha wanted no part of a peace that would deny him triumph and high regard, as these actions demonstrated, for not only did Mustapha enhance his reputation as a military leader to be feared and respected through his bold action at Famagusta, he made it next to impossible for the Europeans to put any trust in a diplomatic solution to their conflict with the Ottoman Empire. He also gained the good opinion of Selim as a relentless champion of Islam. In a single treacherous act, Lala Mustapha had guaranteed himself a preeminent military role in the war with Europe and subverted any chance at non-military resolution. That he also made himself a loathed target for European officers seems to have had no impact upon him.

The immediate benefit to Mustapha for his treatment of the Venetians of Famagusta was a spectacular upsurge in his reputation as a fierce defender of his faith and a loyal fighter for the Sultan. His long delay at conquest was forgotten, and he was once again seen as a valiant soldier. The Europeans might be appalled by what Mustapha did, but he was seen as daring and heroic by the more gung-ho of the Ottoman military leaders. Men like Sokolli were reluctant to speak out against what Mustapha had done, no matter how much they were maintaining the righteous conduct of Islam—the political climate was such that for a soldier to set aside the moral teachings of his faith and justify it by military exigencies was not only acceptable, it was laudable, and Mustapha knew it.

But Lala Mustapha badly underestimated the Venetian response to these reprehensible events, for they were not cowed and terrified, as it was assumed they would be—they were furious, and that fury drove them into the Holy League with all the strength of their wrath, reactions that surprised many Ottoman officers, who had been taught to consider mercy a virtue only in Allah, and a sign of cowardice in men. When fighting men behaved with pity, the Ottoman interpretation was that the men had had a loss of nerve. Many acts of Europeans, intended to help create fellowship with the enemy, instead were seen as indications that the Europeans were lily-livered, and deserved defeat and disgrace. That the Venetians would not concede the campaign to them by virtue of arms and ferocity seemed inconceivable; it took crucial time for the Ottoman forces to comprehend the infuriated state of the Venetians, and Venice used that time to advantage.

Since they had already committed themselves to the Pope's war—as many Venetians called the proposed campaign before the fall of Famagusta—they saw the betrayal at Cyprus as wholly acceptable justification for the war, and rather than back off from direct confrontation, the Maggior Consiglio was at last united in their cause against the Ottoman Empire, and was now out for vengeance. Venice had come to realize that they were a target of Ottoman aggression, and that they would need the aid and support of most of Europe if they were to survive the Turkish attacks. Since Venetian relations with various Hapsburg territories were far from affable, the rallying point provided by the Pope eased their dealings with the powerful dynasty, and offered a degree of protection from Hapsburg ambitions as well.

In another display of diplomatic abjuration of previous agreements not to extend a military presence beyond the Aegean and Mediterranean Seas, the Sultan ordered that what had been a small merchants' port under a protective battlement above a small bay on the Gulf of Patmas in Greece with easy access to the Adriatic Sea be reinforced and made into a naval forward station. The Sultan had made it clear that he intended to control the Adriatic, and Venice along with it, and this harbor-fortress was the first step in his direct challenge to Venice itself, for here the Ottoman ships could lie in safe harbor in a position difficult to attack, and from that vantage point could easily prey upon the Venetian merchant ships and their escorts. The improved naval fortress had been under Venetian control until 1499; it was called Lepanto.

12

EUROPEAN PREPARATION

LL THROUGH THE spring of 1571, the Holy League had been making ready for the coming assault on Ottoman naval power, but the progress had been uneven as egos and agendas clashed, and temperament got ahead of strategy. More than once the fragile alliance looked ready to unravel, requiring all manner of ingenious solutions to diminish the internal clashing among the various officers in the fleet. For the time being, the Ottomans were far off, and the old rivalries were in full flower.

Each nation had taken a stance that put itself as the obvious leader of the fight, and because of that, agreeing on even so minor a thing as preferential war galley design became an issue of contention, as did who would serve aboard which ships, and what position those ships would occupy. The Spanish galleys, for example, were larger than the Venetians', and not as easily handled, but they carried more and heavier guns. That made some of the high-ranking officers prefer the Spanish ships to the Venetians', in spite of the superior range of the Venetian guns, thanks to the slightly raised decks of their war galleys. In addition, some of the Genoese were convinced that the Ottomans knew too much about Venetian ship design, and therefore the Venetian ships would be preferential targets for the Turks. Bickering on these points and many similar ones went on steadily through the initial arrangements for their campaign.

Fortunately, aside from the various holy Orders involved in the preparations, uniforms as such did not yet exist; the tendency was more for soldiers to wear the colors of their company—this was especially crucial to the volunteers—or their country (red and gold for Venetians, gold and black for Spaniards, purple for the Papal States' soldiers, blue and silver for Genoese, and so forth). Soldiers who had done well liked to dress more grandly than their less successful comrades, and so any company of fighters would present a fairly diverse appearance, aside from the colors they shared. Those colors could be in the main garments, in sashes, in armbands, or even in plumes on a hat—the last fairly rare. Had the European commanders been able to debate uniforms as well as all the rest, the fleet might never have left Messina.

Even matters of routine supply got caught in these various rivalries; by the time the ships of the Holy League were sent to the rendezvous, officers on Genoese ships were disinclined to purchase foodstuffs from local markets, preferring instead to be brought "authentic" Genoese food and wine from home by groups of merchants pledged to continue to supply the Genoese fleet while it was lying at Messina. Sicilian and Neapolitan merchants took this conduct amiss, and made a point of serving common Genoese seamen bad wine and poor quality food when the men were ashore.

In the hope of providing a good example to the maritime warriors, Pope Pius V ordered that chaplains for the troops of the Holy League should be taken from all religious Orders, as a means of ensuring political impartiality from the spiritual advisors, as well as a more balanced approach to the fighting men. But politics was in the mix from the start, and with a determined rancor that touched every officer in the fleet. Early in the project, Felipe II had insinuated that Captain General Marcantonio Colonna was an unwilling participant in the proceedings, reluctant to do his duty, which deeply offended Colonna—and not without cause. Eventually this incident was relegated to a matter of misunderstanding and set right with the intervention of Francisco Borgia, the aged and ailing Superior General of the Jesuits, but a faint, burnt flavor of rancor remained, particularly when—with an eye to appeasing powerful Spanish interests—Felipe's bastard half-brother was given command of the naval forces of the Holy League by the Council of Trent. Don Juan of Austria finally had something to do.

Felipe was officially pleased with the arrangement, but he also sent letters to various leaders in the Holy League, cautioning them about Don Juan, reminding them of his youth and inexperience, but also driving in the point that Spain controlled the League, and that the Church and Spain were equally joined in this campaign. By the time Don Juan heard Mass at Montserrat and boarded his ship at Barcelona, he had to deal with buzzing rumors of his incompetence and unreliability. Don Juan's command was further undermined by Felipe's official insistence that every order Don Juan issued had to be countersigned by Luis de Requesens, who had commanded the Spanish fleet during the Morisco War. This was supposedly because de Requesens was instructing Don Juan in the fine points of military seamanship, but in actuality reduced Don Juan's authority, just as Felipe intended. So long as Don Juan had to ask for approval, the final authority for the whole campaign resided in Felipe's grasp as King of Spain and leader of the Spanish Empire.

Felipe had a number of other conditions attached to Don Juan's leadership, including an example of family spite: Don Juan was only to be addressed as His Excellency, not His Highness. He was also to proceed only with the approval of his senior commanders—Giannandrea Doria of Genoa, Don Alvaro de Bazan of Spain, Marcantonio Colonna of Rome and Naples, Don Juan de Cardona of Sicily, and Sebastian Venier and Agostino Barbarigo of Venice. Most of these men had a great deal of experience fighting the Ottomans and were feeling the Turkish expansion as an imminent threat, which made them willing to hold their personal animosities at bay while they took on the Ottomans for their mutual benefit. There was a bit of a crimp to these provisions: Felipe required that the Genoese support the Spanish ships preferentially in battle, an order that exacerbated the resentment simmering between Doria and Venier, and strained the relationships between the various participants.

Because of these galling restrictions placed upon him, Don Juan undertook a crash course in naval warfare, consulting not only his senior commanders but Don Garcia de Toledo, a once highly regarded maritime warrior, now disgraced—he had been accused of debauchery and abuse of command, but there are indications that the real reason was more political than these accusations would suggest, and that Don Garcia had wholly fallen from favor at Felipe's court—and living in Italy, a semi-invalid who was ready to join Don Juan if he should ask. (Don Juan declined his offer.) Don Garcia was eager for the fight, and wanted to participate in any way he could. Of all the various officers and advisors, Don Garcia was the only man advising Don Juan who did not have a political agenda to support, and who called Felipe's and Doria's inclination to preserve European galleys at all costs a sure road to disaster, all in the name of minimizing the need for battle. "The battle has come to us, and we must fight or perish," Don Garcia wrote to Don Juan in June. "It will take emphatic action to win."

The rendezvous for the Holy League ships was Messina in Sicily, and it was there at the end of summer that the fleet gathered. Venice, although being harried throughout the Adriatic by Ottoman corsairs and war galleys, supplied the largest number of ships—105 standard war galleys and six larger, more formidable galleasses, measuring 160 feet in length and slightly more than forty feet abeam, carrying sixty oars manned by five or six men each, carrying fourteen front-mounted and fourteen aft-mounted guns on raised platforms. This is what gave the galleass its value in battle, since its size made it clumsy, with regular cannon to augment the larger guns on the platforms at the fore and midship, their complement numbering almost eighty cannon per ship. There were also twenty-five *fregate* (scout ships) and a dozen or so round ships to carry supplies. The Spanish galleys— larger and less maneuverable than the Venetians'—numbered eighty- one, carrying between forty and fifty cannon apiece. Twelve galleys were supplied by the Pope; Tuscany sent seven galleys from Pisa, the oars manned by hired oarsmen, not convicts, according to the official account; the Maltese Knights of Saint John, Savoy, and Genoa sup- plied three galleys apiece. Another twenty-five *fregate* and ten round ships completed the fleet. By the time the fleet was ready to depart, it numbered 213 fighting ships, roughly sixty scouting and courier craft of various sorts, and another two dozen support-and-supply ships.

Unlike the Turks, the Europeans were not only armed with can- non, they had arquebuses, an early form of a rifle; personal firearms were rarely used by Ottoman soldiers, aside from occasional ornate pistols, but arquebuses were becoming standard for Europeans for their greater penetrating power: Turkish bows could fire much faster than arquebuses, but at any distance at all, the arrows could not pierce European body-armor, while arquebus balls could take out a soldier with a single hit, more than making up for their slowness in firing. During the supplying of the fighting men in the European fleet, arquebuses were given particular attention—soldiers who knew how to use firearms were assigned to crucial positions on the ships in order to take as much advantage as possible of the superior penetra- tion of these important new weapons. Round ships carrying supplies were loaded with gunpowder and balls for the arquebuses as well as the cannon.

Doria, although far from encouraging the coming battle, made an excellent recommendation for using the arquebuses; he pointed out that the galleasses were too high for deck-to-deck boarding, and given that the galleasses were predominantly being used as gunnery platforms for the heavy cannon, the midship could be used to hold

arquebusiers. Their shots would carry farther from the higher elevation of the galleasses and would keep the shooters in a more protected location than on the decks of most of the war galleys. He also
suggested unshipping the metal beaks at the front of the galleasses to
allow the cannon to fire directly forward. Galleasses were too lum-
bering to be able to do much ramming in any case, and this way what
might be a disadvantage could be changed to a useful adaptation. Don
Juan gave the recommendations his consideration, and decided to
employ both of them. Doria might not like fighting, but he had a
first-class strategic mind.

Along with arquebuses, the Europeans had another innovation for
the hard business of battle—boarding nets, which would make both
boarding and later towing less dangerous. The Europeans knew how
to throw and climb the boarding nets, which gave them an edge in
terms of actual combat, for the nets could serve as barrier as much as
provide access. They had the additional advantage that the Ottoman
fighting men had little experience with boarding nets, and would be
unlikely to use them to the Ottoman benefit. The Turks had lines for
boarding, and small planks, but both the lines and boards could prove
more hazardous than useful, particularly in the heat of battle; boards
could be jarred or overset and lines could tangle or swing beyond the
intended limits, and jumping from deck to deck, no matter how close
the ships were, was simply too dangerous for any but the most hard-
ened fighters. Nets tended to stay where they belonged and were
flexible enough for a soldier to maintain safe footing while clamber-
ing from one ship to another. The boarding nets were recognized almost at once as the superior devices they were.

Because of the complicated command arrangements, as well as internal dissension, the fleet was unable to leave port until September
16. When they finally did move out from Messina, observers described the forest of masts and the grand appearance of the banners
and sails with an emotion approaching awe. In a report sent to the

Pope, an Ambrosian monk from Palermo declared, "Surely they fly on the wings of angels to do the Savior's bidding." As overblown as this sentiment might be, it served to sum up the public view of the mission the Holy League had undertaken.

With the Papal Nuncio standing on the jetty to bless each ship as it sailed into the dawn, the Holy League's navy was finally on its way, and the fleet was at least as much a public relations display as a serious military venture, since they were proceeding on sketchy intelligence and had no specific plan of attack. Another and far more treacherous factor to their campaign was that by setting out so late in the year, they were risking storms, which would do them no good, but it had been tacitly acknowledged that the various countries involved would not be likely to sustain their cooperation into the next year, so it was now or never. Felipe of Spain might well change his mind about cooperating with the Venetians, and that would be the end of this cobbled-together navy. It was unlikely that common cause could be sustained through the winter.

So with Don Juan's flagship, the 70-oar Spanish war galley *Real*, carrying 410 oarsmen and an equal number of crew and fighting men, at the head of the fleet, the Europeans set out to find the Ottomans. Behind the *Real* came Venier under the banner of the Lion of Saint Mark of Venice, and Marcantonio Colonna, bearing the banners of the Pope and Naples. The banner of the Holy League itself was yet to be unfurled. For the time being the various groups among the Europeans had managed to set aside their differences and unite against their common enemy. Their original intention had been to relieve Cyprus, but, although they did not know it yet, that was no longer possible: Famagusta had fallen. The European fleet learned of the tragedy a few days later, when it was the capstone on their motivation for Lepanto. For now, strengthened in their purpose, the Europeans turned toward Corfu, where the Ottomans were reported to be raiding.

13

COMPLICATIONS

WHILE LALA MUSTAPHA was stepping up his efforts at the walls of Famagusta, Ottoman ships had focused much of their energies on Venice. Although treaties specifically protected La Serenissima from Turkish attack, this provision was increasingly viti-ated by corsairs who not only stepped up predation on the merchant marine but included attacks on the city itself. Most Venetian men armed themselves whenever they stepped outside, and a series of for-tifications were commenced on the Giudecca and on the islands to the immediate east of the Arsenal, and small cannon were set in place on the walls of the Arsenal. In June and July, Turkish ships came within sight of San Marco's Byzantine domes, and one small Ot-toman squadron under Kara Hodja managed a brief blockade of the Bacino di San Marco. Never in all Venice's millennium of history had the city sustained such a long period of direct, nautical military threat as it did in 1570 and 1571.

For most of the summer the Holy League struggled to agree on strategies, the pressure from the Pope became more insistent, and as discouraging reports were dispatched from Venice and Cyprus, the Spanish became more hesitant about an all-out attack even while the official position of Felipe was faithful support of the Pope. Gian-nandrea Doria, endorsing the policies of Felipe II, was most reluc-tant of all to pursue a direct attack, but recommended a more cautious approach, which, predictably, incited the ire of the Venetians, who stood to lose the most by such delays.

The Turks, buoyed up by their success at Cyprus, were becoming more bellicose throughout the Adriatic, making for Corfu and the Venetian holdings along the Dalmatian coast, extending their presence well into the crucial trading lanes that made Venice the economic dynamo it was. This pattern of incursions troubled Doria, who had no wish to risk Spanish ships defending Venetian territory, a reservation shared by many of the non-Venetian members of the Holy League.

But the agreed-upon purpose of the campaign was to stop the Ottoman navy from coming farther into European territory, and to preserve what claims now existed on islands and coastal regions that were marked by the Ottomans for takeover. Had not the Famagusta siege been so prolonged, and had it not ended so heinously, it is unlikely that the Europeans could have reached sufficient accord to attempt their united push against Ottoman incursions, but public awareness had been taken by Famagusta, and opinion rallied to the maintaining of Venetian lands, seeing the challenge to Venice as a not-so-veiled threat to all of Europe. The European flotilla did not learn of Famagusta's loss until they had set to sea, bound for the Adriatic; they were informed on the eve of Lepanto, and when news came, the Europeans were appalled and incensed.

On October 4, another problem arose on Sebastian Venier's galley: a number of Spanish officers made derogatory comments to some of the Venetians serving under Venier, which led to a minor riot, and a handful of men were killed in the resultant mayhem. Venier, to make a point, had the Spaniards hanged from the mastheads. When Don Juan learned of this acrimonious series of misadventures, he became furious and was on the brink of having Venier put in chains, an action that would have banished what little comity existed among the various fighting forces had he pursued it. Fortunately, Colonna kept his head and encouraged Don Juan to set such grievances aside until after they had won the battle. Don Juan saw the sense in this, but from that time on, he held Venier at arm's length, and only dealt with the prickly Venetian through seconds-in-command. He had no desire to be accused of favoring Venetians over other members of the Holy League.

There were similar skirmishes among other crews in the European ships, but none of them seem to have resulted in death, and so they were deemed of minor importance. In terms of the military goals associated with this endeavor, it was important to keep regional and nationalisitic squabbles out of the European mix as far as possible, but rivalries are stubborn, and it was apparent to the senior officers that keeping their forces united in purpose was likely to be as hard a thing as beating the Turks. Disciplinary measures against violent squabbles were enacted in hopes of putting an end to the hostilities, but there were still occasional problems that cropped up fairly frequently, requiring swift responses in order to contain the damage they brought about.

At various of their war councils, a number of military expectations that had been laid out in accord with national interests came into sharp relief, along with personality clashes among the senior officers. Don Juan himself was supposed to put Spanish interests ahead of other European interests. So he found himself subject to criticism when he sometimes sided with the Venetians, preferring their boldness to Spanish circumspection, as it was more in his character to do. Along with the Venetians, Don Juan wanted to mount a direct attack on Ali Pasha's supply line by conducting a destructive raid on Negroponte, which would not only disrupt Ottoman communications, it might drive Ali Pasha out from the protection of Lepanto where his ships would be as exposed as the Europeans' were. Only Don Juan's excellent understanding of the stakes they played for kept him from ordering the assault he and the Venetians favored, deciding instead to do his best to build consensus among the members of the Holy League while pursuing a single confrontation with Ali Pasha.

But with heavy weather coming on, Don Juan had to act or leave the seas until spring, at which time the stresses already working against the Europeans might well have gone beyond the breaking point, and all that would be left would be ongoing bickering while the Ottoman navy swept down upon Europe, so Don Juan pledged to engage the enemy in battle before the weather turned. He admitted that the Ottoman ships were in greater number than his, but he believed that "God and fine seamanship," as he wrote to Don Garcia de Toledo, would deliver the victory. Issuing rosaries to all Christian oarsmen, and keeping non-Christian oarsmen on shortened chains at their oars, the fleet turned toward the Corinth Channel and the Gulf of Patmas.

14

OTTOMAN PREPARATION

ROUGHLY A WEEK before the Holy League fleet set out from Messina, but after it had reached almost full strength, a singular event took place—at least according to persistent rumor—a black-painted-and-sailed Ottoman galley slipped past the ships in the harbor; the corsair Kara Hodja (sometimes called Karakoch) had come to have a covert look at the European ships, and having seen most of what the Europeans had to offer, he sped back toward the Ottoman navy, prepared to give them an account of all he had learned—that the European fleet was roughly half the size of the Ottoman fleet, and somewhat in disarray, short of oarsmen and inadequate to the challenge set by the Turks.

This was, in fact, an incorrect estimate, for although the European fleet was smaller than the Ottoman fleet, it was also about thirty percent larger than Kara Hodja counted, a difference that proved to be significant when the two navies finally met. It may be that in staying beyond sight of the watchmen on the European ships, Kara Hodja made an inaccurate count, or it may be he did not want to report what his superiors did not wish to hear. Or he may have not wanted to linger in European waters, and so did only a cursory survey in order to ensure a clean getaway. Whatever the reason for the inaccurate intelligence, it did not provide the degree of advantage it had been assumed it would, for although the Ottoman ships were greater in number than the European ships, they were not sufficient to drive the

Europeans off by a show of force alone, as some of the Ottoman officers supposed.

Whatever the reason for the error, the count he received was good
news to Ali Pasha, the commander of the Ottoman fleet. Young, impetuous, daring, and ambitious, he had gained a fine reputation in his
short career, and that, in turn, had inspired him to greater feats. He
had a lot to live up to, and he was determined not only to do that, but
to accomplish more than was expected of him. Success in the Sultan's
cause was a sure path to high position and riches, and Ali had taken
up Selim's cause as his own. Yet in spite of all his promise, Ali had had
a difficult summer, attempting to take Crete from Venetian hands,
but without success. Marcantonio Quirini—the same man who had
got through to resupply Cyprus—was defending Crete, and did so so
successfully that Ali and his galleys were unable to land on the island.

To improve morale and strengthen the Ottoman navy still further,
Ali set about kidnapping Venetians and loyal peasants to be oarsmen
on his galleys, so by the time the Holy League was gathering at
Messina, Ali's ships had 7,000 new Venetian and Venetian-Greek
oarsmen to move his ships into battle with the Europeans. He also
had the support and participation of the corsair Uchiali, who, with
his shallow-draft galliots, was able to operate much closer to shore
than galleys could. Only when Quirini was ordered by the Maggior
Consiglio to abandon his present position and join the fleet at
Messina did Ali have any chance of successfully conquering Crete.

Just when it seemed that Crete could be conquered, Ali was ordered by the Sultan himself to move away from Crete to Little Gallipoli, as Lepanto was often called by the Turks. Selim was certain
that the Greek islands still remaining in Venetian control would
shortly be within the easy grasp of Ottoman forces without the time-
consuming bother of actual siege, and so the islands could be strategi-
cally set aside while the Europeans were driven off the seas. Just at
present, the Sultan wanted all the European ships destroyed. Selim

saw the narrow Corinth Channel leading into the Gulf of Patmas as an excellent protection for his navy to use against the European ships, which must be exposed to attack from the land while passing down the Corinth Channel, and had to face the fortress guns once they reached the gulf. By placing the bulk of his navy at Lepanto, Selim could use it and his other fortress at Negroponte to keep up pressure on Venice and the Greek islands in Venetian control without being in danger of sailing beyond Ottoman supply lines or Ottoman safe harbors. Although the Sultan never got around to ordering more cannon emplacements along the Corinth Channel as he had indicated he would do, he did set up a number of observation posts leading into the Gulf of Patmas, with the intention of having first class and up-to-date information on European ships in the region.

With the weather turning inclement about ten days earlier than usual, Ali Pasha allowed himself to be persuaded that the Europeans would not risk fighting before spring, and he made arrangements for repairs and improvements to begin on his ships at once, confident that there would be more advantage in making the most of the bad weather than in keeping ready for a battle that could not happen until winter was over.

Sending his sick and wounded ashore, Ali Pasha prepared to winter at Lepanto, and had the intention of stepping up attacks on Venice in the spring after using the winter to repair his ships, mount heavier guns, and capture more slaves to man the oars of his galleys. At Lepanto, he had the advantage of a well-protected harbor, defensive fortifications, a battery of cannon, and ample food, munitions, and materiel for his troops. Once the winter faded, he would be in an excellent position to mount major assaults on not only Venice and Venetian territory, but Naples, Sicily, the Papal States, and the south coast of Spain. Ali, as the commander of the naval force, was in a position to realize fame and fortune as well as political clout from his next few years of determined warfare—every politician and soldier from Rome to Constantinople knew it, even though Ali had an impressive array of political rivals and out-and-out enemies.

Remaining away from the Sultan's court until he had secured an undisputed victory seemed the wisest course to Ali, who informed Sokolli that he would not undertake any long voyage before spring, when he would order his ships to Venice. This was a bold boast, and it meant that Ali was setting his bar very high, but he knew that without a major triumph, he would have to accommodate the demands not only of the Sultan but of the various political cliques in the Divan, which might well prove more dangerous to Ali personally than any strategy devised by the Europeans.

The one thing that worried Ali Pasha was that he was unsure where the European fleet was: the ships had struck out across the mouth of the Adriatic, and now, being out of sight of land, could not readily be found. Ali sent out scouting ships to try to find the Holy League ships without themselves becoming lost, with the intention of setting a trap for the Europeans, who had *fregate* out searching for Ali and the Ottoman navy. Had it not been such a deadly game, the searches-within-searches might well have been funny.

15

FINDING THE FOE

AFTER THREE DAYS of casting about futilely in search of the Ottoman ships, Don Juan sent out one of the Knights of Malta, Gil d'Andrade, who had almost fifteen years' experience fighting the Turks at sea. He was given a quartet of fast, double-oared galleys and headed out in front of the Europeans, determined to learn if Ali Pasha had gone to Lepanto, as had been rumored, or whether he was making for the Sea of Marmora and winter anchorage, as Doria and some of the older naval officers believed he would do. While d'Andrade kept up the search, Don Juan's fleet entered the harbor at Corfu after fending off an attack by the ships Ali had left behind to keep the island from being reinforced by Venice.

The island had been wrecked by Ali's men, apparently punishing Corfu for failing to surrender the fortress. The scale of destruction was beyond what many of the men on the European ships had seen. After Famagusta, the devastation on Corfu only served to underscore the bitterness of the Europeans toward the Turks, and the degree of wrath the Turks felt toward the Europeans.

Fishermen and other sea-goers were stopped by the European fleet and interrogated in the hope that the movements of the Ottoman navy could be learned without the fleet having to come within firing range to obtain crucial information. One of the reports they were given suggested that the Ottoman navy had been divided, and half the fleet sent off to Africa for the winter, and although this was a common practice, and one that had been done in the past, many of the European officers did not believe Ali had done it this year, not with most of the naval ships of Europe pursuing him and the honor of the Sultan riding on his decisions. On the whole, it seemed likely that the Ottoman forces would not split their fleet at so critical a period of aggression as this, for it would be too reckless a move even for as impetuous a young man as Ali Pasha.

The weather, always a factor, was beginning to take a toll on the oarsmen, and some of the soldiers as well. The oarsmen, kept at their oars twenty-four hours a day, seven days a week, on benches on the outriggers, hanging off the sides of the galleys, were exposed to everything that came along: storms, heat, waves, wind. Many of them were showing symptoms of frostbite from the cold, squally weather, and they had to be relieved from constant rowing, or be lost. The soldiers, many of whom had to sleep on the open deck in simple bedrolls, also suffered from rain and cold. Even the officers, allocated cabins of their own, were usually damp and cold, just as in summer they would have suffered from stifling heat. The reality of the conditions of this voyage was constantly being borne in on Don Juan and his commanders, complicating their already complex situation.

There were debates still raging among the Europeans, mostly about how the Ottomans were to be stopped. Doria and the Spanish were in favor of island-hopping, reclaiming European control as a means of building up bases from which they could worry the Ottoman ships within their range of supplies. Other possibilities had to be considered, however, in light of the precarious nature of the Holy League itself, which was not designed to be an ongoing federation.

For the reasons created by the structure of the Holy League, Don Juan, against the orders of his half-brother, Felipe II, favored a single, hard, swift strike at the Ottoman navy. Not surprisingly, Doria was against it. But after the sight of Corfu and the news from Cyprus, several of the senior officers had come to favor Don Juan's approach:

Barbarigo, Santa Cruz, and Colonna had all come around to support staking all on a single battle. They knew they had one chance now, and if they did not take advantage of it, months would go by before they could strike again. Doria and the more cautious officers favored a symbolic strike on a minor Turkish outpost for form's sake, and then they thought that going to winter anchorage would be wisest. The debate was becoming rancorous when d'Andrade returned with his four galleys to report that Ali Pasha had indeed withdrawn to Lepanto and seemed to be preparing to winter there. This was the impetus needed to swing the balance in favor of driving the Ottoman ships from the shelter of the fortress of Lepanto and into the Gulf of Patmas for a showdown.

At Lepanto, the council of war Ali called was no more unanimous than the ones Don Juan endured: the corsairs, while faithful to the Sultan, were not inclined to fight massed naval battles. They did not like risking their own ships in such a contest. Uchiali's stock was low with the Turks just then—he had guessed wrong about the European fleet, predicting that it would not put to sea until spring. He backed a plan for ongoing raids through the winter, in which he was supported by Hassan, the son of the famous corsair Barbarossa, who was worried about the political shenanigans going on in Constantinople as much as the military efforts of the Europeans. He believed it would be better to wait until matters were settled at court before the corsairs were asked to risk their ships unnecessarily. But Hassan also knew the Sultan wanted the European fleet destroyed, and so he advised taking time to add even more ships to the Ottoman navy so they could deliver a decisive defeat to the Holy League, settling the control of the seas once and for all. He considered the Holy League to be a hodgepodge of conflicting interests and internal jealousies. "Pick at their flanks," he advised, "and they will tear themselves apart. All we need do is seize the bones."

On the advice of Hassan, Ali Pasha ordered that all the oarsmen be close-chained to their oars and told that there would be no release, so that if the ship went down, the galley slaves would drown. This meant the kind of motivation that the oarsmen would understand, and that Christian, Muslim, or Jew, they would strive to keep their ship afloat at all costs as a means of staying alive. Only when the actual fighting was about to begin did Ali change his mind and promise his galley slaves their freedom if they won the day, but by then the galley slaves were not inclined to trust the Ottoman officers.

The scouts sent to find the Europeans returned with an inconclusive report—yes, the Europeans were coming—no, they had not been able to locate them—yes, the Europeans knew about the Ottoman raids on the coast—no, they had not announced a plan for fighting the Ottomans, not yet. Caution appeared to be the wisest stance for the time being, since no one, not even Ali himself, wanted to stick his neck out.

Mahomet Sirocco was another who advocated avoiding direct battle. He was an old and experienced sailor who saw the virtue of using the winter to shore up their fleet; he did not support the idea of stepping up action against the Europeans while the weather was bad, for he saw too many chances for trouble. No matter how much of an advantage the Ottoman ships had, it could always be better, and if the Europeans should find them and insist on drawing them out into battle, the Egyptian believed they would lose oarsmen no matter what, and that would require more raiding during the stormy season to get slaves to man their oars, another foolish hazard. He sided with most of the officers, and used his long experience to support his caveats.

Eager as he was for battle, Ali understood all the hesitation and doubt that filled his officers' council, but he had one overriding consideration, one that trumped all other cards in anyone's hand—an order directly from the Sultan commanding Ali to fight and sink the European fleet if it came near enough to make such an attack possible. Selim wanted Ali to make an example of the Holy League, so that no such federation would ever rise again to threaten Ottoman authority on the seas, and European ships would not dare to set out onto the sea. Once the European fleet was destroyed—and no other result but utter European destruction was even considered—Selim expected his ships to converge upon all Venetian territory, from the Greek Islands to the Venetian lagoon, and from there to launch land-based attacks on the Italian peninsula culminating in the conquest of Rome and the humiliation of the Pope. This official command ended all debate, and the Ottoman officers set about provisioning their ships for battle.

Ali had 25,000 soldiers in the fortress; he decided to put most of them aboard the ships rather than keeping them in the fortress, for although Lepanto had cannon to protect the harbor, once the fighting moved out of range, the gunners would be worse than useless. Ali had no intention of providing such an advantage to the Europeans. His ships would bristle with soldiers and cannon. He had enough time to prepare for the arrival of the Holy League and he intended to make the most of it. By the time the European ships hove into sight, the fight would be only a formality to ensure Ottoman victory.

16

THE POINT OF NO RETURN

THE NIGHT OF Friday, October 5, the European fleet was anchored in Viscando harbor. The wind was rising and blustery,
another signal for an early beginning to the storms of winter—not
the best of omens, and, like all sailors, the Europeans watched the
omens carefully, and read the sky for signs morning and night. While
many of the officers in the Holy League were uneasy about the hint of
a storm on the air, Don Juan's enthusiasm was undaunted: with the
weather turning, the Ottomans would not expect an attack, and that
would ensure the Europeans had the advantage of surprise. He
stepped up the soldiers' drill in preparation for the battle ahead, and
he summoned his officers to set the plan for the battle.

At first light, the Sicilian Don Juan de Cardona was given eight
double-ranked light galleys selected for speed and sent off toward
Lepanto to ascertain the position of the Ottoman ships, and, if possible, the number of them. While de Cardona was gone, Don Juan de
Austria finished setting out the formation from which they would begin to fight, and though Don Juan went through the motions of complying with Felipe's orders, he was by now sufficiently in charge that
he was not likely to have his orders double-checked; counter-signing
might do at Messina, but with the Ottomans not far ahead, such per-
snickety details were recognized as being unnecessarily complicated,
and therefore against the best interests of the Europeans.

The Holy League ships followed after de Cardona, not nearly as swiftly, taking care not to exhaust the oarsmen, for their strength was likely to be the most essential element of the coming battle. Even those captains who demanded a lot of the men propelling their ships knew that exhausted oarsmen were dangerous to everyone, and so kept to the stately pace set by the flagship, during which time Christian oarsmen were unchained from their oars and were issued weapons, and non-Christian oarsmen were close-chained to the oars: with fighting so near at hand, everyone had to be reckoned a participant.

As Don Juan traveled toward Lepanto, he busied himself with establishing the battle formations that they would soon have to employ. Anticipating an exposed left, he assigned most of the left to the Venetians under Agostino Barbarigo, with command of the far end of the left going to the audacious Marcantonio Quirini, for these tough merchant-captains had years of experience maneuvering in combat with Ottoman ships, and he knew he could rely on their expertise, to say nothing of their eagerness for vengeance for Cyprus. There were sixty-three war galleys in the Venetian contingent. Each division would be headed by a galleass, its heavy guns trained dead ahead, into the faces of the Ottomans. The left galleasses would be under the commands of Ambrosio and Antonio Bragadin, who had good reason to want to take on the Ottomans, and the inclination to go the extra length in battle.

On the right were the Genoese under Giannandrea Doria, and the Spanish, the Neapolitans, the Sicilians, the Tuscans, and the other smaller contingents. A bit more of a mixed bag, the right was just the type of assorted Europeans that the Ottomans so decried. It was also a group that might fret under Doria's cautious nature. Weapons were more varied on the right, and the round ships managing supplies were ordered to keep close watch on the right, since the broad requirements of the fighters made supply more crucial than among the more uniform weapons of the Venetians.

These ships on the right were also where most of the volunteer fighting men were stationed, including Don Juan's kinsman and old court friend, Alessandro Farnese, who had his own company of 200 with him. There were also a handful of French soldiers, and a group of Orthodox Greeks who had fled Cyprus when Lala Mustapha invaded, all of whom had come to help stop the Ottoman advance. The comrades of Farnese, the French, and the Orthodox Greeks did not have galleys of their own, and so took up their posts where Don Juan assigned them. There were a few volunteers with their own ships, or with sufficient experience at command to be given the captaincy of leased galleys from Venice, Spain, and Genoa. Three galleys on the right were commanded by the former English pirate Sir Thomas Stukeley, one of the more prominent independent captains fighting with the Holy League. A capable seaman, Stukeley was motivated as much by greed as by religious fervor, and was quite candid about it. "If God will give us the victory, He will also give us rewards," he remarked to Doria's officers. He had good reason for such hopes, for most corsairs carried their accumulated loot in the holds of their galleys, making them very desirable prizes indeed.

At the center was the *Real,* Don Juan's flagship, with a line of sixty-four war galleys around it, most of them Spanish, but a few Venetian, and a handful of Papal ships. This was the heart of the Holy League naval forces, and it was the place where the Ottoman ships would have to strike hardest. By having the center mixed, Don Juan felt confident that the rest of the European ships would be diligent in protecting the center, no matter what the political climate might be, for at least one of the galleys in the center represented each of the member states of the Holy League. This mix also reminded all the commanders that they all stood to share in the victory they sought.

On the right-center was Marcantonio Colonna for Naples and the Pope, as steady and diplomatic as ever. He supervised the order of ships' squadrons as they moved through the Corinth Channel, making for the gulf and the Turkish ships. At the rear of the European ships came the round supply ships, the *fregate,* and a reserve of thirty war galleys under Santa Cruz that were assigned to fill in where the fighting was most tempestuous, and to shore up weakened places in the line. Even as the ships slipped toward their battle lines, Doria strove to convince Don Juan to turn back, sparing ships and lives to fight later, in the spring, when they would have fair winds and calm seas for their fighting.

The wind was brisk the night of Saturday, October 6. Ottoman scouts—undetected by the European scouts and watchmen—brought news of the European ships coming, and Ali took advantage of this to begin to move his war galleys out from Lepanto, into a massive line making a barricade across the gulf. He was careful not to order his ships into too extended a line, where they might have to fight in the open, unprotected by Ottoman reserves, but he managed to string his ships out in a long, curving arc that reached almost from shore to shore, limiting the area of the gulf where the Europeans could prosecute the battle. Ali was prepared to follow the Sultan's orders, but he was not going to take foolish chances. He wanted his victory to be as far from Pyrrhic as possible, and he begrudged the Europeans every ship under his command. When the sun rose on Sunday the seventh, Ali had deployed almost all of his 274 warships, 206 of which were galleys, and all of which were in a formidable crescent of ship and sail.

Turning against the wind toward the Ottoman fleet, the Europeans celebrated Mass, only the intonations of the priests serving as counterpoint to the steady dip of the oars. The men on the Holy League ships were silent except for the responses to the religious rite as they came around into the Gulf of Patmas and headed down the waterway toward the Turks, less than twenty miles ahead of them. Shortly after Mass was over, the Europeans caught sight of the Ottomans ahead. Almost at once the Ottoman sailors and fighting men burst into shouts; they banged their shields with their weapons, and they called upon Allah to vanquish their enemies; some of the Janissaries danced on the decks of the Ottoman ships. The Europeans remained silent; not a single shot was fired, not an arrow was loosed as the ships moved down the gulf.

With the European fleet approaching, de Cardona turned his galleys back into the line as the gap between the Ottoman ships and the Holy League steadily closed. Don Juan de Austria went aboard a fast *fregata* and hurried down one arm of the right, to make sure the ships were holding the line and to exhort the men to courage and purpose. He promised the soldiers that God was on their side and would give them the victory—very like what Ali Pasha had promised his oarsmen. On the left, Luis de Requesens did the same as the wind continued to pick up. The three wings of the European ships made slow but steady progress toward the huge display of Ottoman naval power; many of the Europeans admitted later that they thought that their numbers were inadequate to the fight, and hoped that Don Juan would order the Holy League to turn about.

Compensating for the unusual battle formation the Europeans were using, Ali pulled his flagship, *Sultana,* forward in the line and disrupted the arc of ships still further by ordering his flanks back, the better for line-of-fire when the shooting began. He made a point of keeping up the noise to rattle the Europeans, and he ran up the green silk Mecca prayer flag on which Allah was written 28,900 times in gold; this was a treasure of the Sultan's, and a most sacred relic of Islam. Never had this banner been carried in battle when the Ottomans had not won. The ninety-six ships at the Ottoman center ordered their oarsmen to duck under their benches, so as not to provide targets for the Europeans.

Facing the Venetians were the Egyptians, their galliots on the end moving toward the northern Albanian shore in an attempt to get around Quirini to encircle his ships. On the Ottoman left, Uchiali commanded sixty-three war galleys and galliots. Ali kept a reserve of about fifty war galleys and lighter *fregate* to the left rear, ready to fill in and resupply from Lepanto harbor where and when necessary.

Just as the Europeans were completing their moving into position, the wind, which had been at the Ottomans' backs, shifted around to the right-rear of the Europeans. The Ottoman sails came down rapidly, before the ships could be blown too far out of formation, and the oarsmen were ordered out from under their benches and back to their oars. On the European ships, sails were quickly raised to catch the steady breeze as the two navies came together.

17

OPENING MOVES

THE EUROPEAN SILENCE ended when Don Juan took his pistol and fired—although way out of range—directly at Ali Pasha. A Turkish cannon answered the shot; the ball could not cover half the distance to the European ships. The Europeans cheered, and the oarsmen leaned into their tasks with greater determination; with the wind behind them, the European advance picked up speed. One of the Europeans fired a shot in the direction of the Ottoman ships, and was answered with another shot, although neither could as yet reach the other. Don Juan ordered the crucifix banner of the Holy League unfurled, and the Europeans cheered again as their ships surged forward, carried by the rising wind. The gesture was an important one, indicating that the flagship would fight—by no means the usual tactic in naval battles of the period. For pride if no other reason, Ali had to respond in kind, and just as well, for Don Juan ordered his ship be brought alongside *Sultana* as soon as was possible.

The battle began with cannon at around eleven in the morning, and for the first time the Ottoman forces saw what the cumbersome galleasses could do with their forward-mounted guns, and it drove the mockery out of them with the first blasts. All jokes about the beakless huge craft being gelded stopped as the damage potential from the guns was rapidly borne in on the Ottoman officers; they also realized that the slightly higher decks of the Venetian war galleys gave the Europeans a longer range with their guns, and one that could not be

lessened easily so long as the wind was at the Europeans' backs, helping to advance the line without wearing out the oarsmen before the
fighting was even underway. What had seemed a sure victory for the
Ottoman navy now became far less certain as the heavy guns ham-
mered at the Turkish galleys and galliots, breaking the oarsmen's outriggers so that men and oars dangled in the water, and punching holes
in the ships near the waterline.

One of the first shots fired from de Cardona's ship splintered the
ornamental lantern on Ali Pasha's *Sultana,* which was seen as a very
bad omen by the Turks. Ali himself attempted to make a joke of the
devastating shot, remarking, "They are like children, smashing pretty
things," but he also remarked to his officers that he hoped Allah
would permit them to give a good answer to such an audacious question. For the next half hour, that answer eluded Ali as his oarsmen began to struggle against the wind and the constant thunder of the
European guns.

Early in the battle the Ottoman line was breached in several places
as the European cannon continued to create inroads among the
Ottoman ships. The Europeans, well-drilled in gunnery, kept up a
steady rate of fire that at first surprised and then alarmed the Ottoman soldiers. The steady cannon fire was soon augmented by arquebuses firing in volleys into the decks of the Ottoman galleys, the
range of the balls roughly ten percent farther than the range of Ottoman arrows.

Real and *Sultana* inexorably continued on their collision course,
with Colonna's ship keeping pace with *Real* but half a length behind.
In anticipation of their impact, Don Juan danced on the gun-
platform—accounts disagree on whether he performed a hornpipe or
a galliard—then prepared for the crash and the singing hiss of grappling lines that would bind the two ships together amid arrows and
arquebus balls. The courageous Sardinian regiment took to the
boarding nets and swarmed over *Sultana*'s deck, and the hand-to-hand

battle was underway, even as Colonna's ship drove into the Ottoman ship up to the sixth rank of oars. The Sardinians forced the Turks back to the mast once, were pushed back to the bow, but they advanced again up the blood-slippery deck, only to be repulsed once more in a pelting of Turkish arrows, with high injuries among the attackers. The Europeans faltered only a short while, then gathered again.

The third charge by the Sardinians took over Ali's deck from stem to stern and *Sultana* became a prize for the Europeans. During this furious assault, Don Juan was wounded in the leg, an injury he made light of as much to maintain his command unquestioned as to assess the damage done—he knew any hint of infirmity on his part could provide Doria and Felipe's officers an excuse for breaking off the attack. About one in the afternoon, while Don Juan continued to fight, the Sardinians bore down on Ali, eventually striking him in the forehead with an arquebus ball, killing him. Almost at once, a galley slave said to be from Malaga rushed forward to hack off Ali Pasha's head and bear it away to the *Real* as a trophy while the Turkish flagship was overrun and taken in tow by the European forces. Although Ali Pasha's head adorned the afterdeck of *Real* for an hour or so, Don Juan was heard to say it should be flung in the sea, and once *Sultana* was completely taken, it was. Ali Pasha's two sons were captured alive, the Mecca prayer flag was run down and the crucifix banner of the Holy League raised in its place, and the trumpeters ordered to play "Victory." It was a bit premature, but it indicated the general tenor of the battle: the Europeans seized the advantage and never let go.

Demoralizing as the loss of the Ottoman leader was, the battle was just in its early stages. On the north side of the gulf, where Mahomet Sirocco's Egyptians faced the Venetians under Quirini and Venier, the greater number of ships in the Ottoman line were attempting to get around behind the Venetian wing, encircle the ships, and sink them. In defiance, Sebastian Venier fired his blunderbuss directly into the faces of the approaching Egyptians and the battle erupted,

Venetian ships firing their cannon on the upward roll to make the most of their extended range, although in a short time the ships were close enough to begin to jockey for boarding. The fighting was desperate: Agostino Barbarigo was wounded in the eye by a Turkish arrow during the first phase of the attack and had to turn over his command to his first officer. The Venetians renewed their efforts, shouting "Famagusta!" as they repulsed the Ottoman ships, forcing them away from their flank even as they attempted to rescue fighting men and unchained oarsmen from six sinking Venetian war galleys.

As the fighting among the Venetians and the Egyptians grew more intense, the smaller number of Venetian war galleys lost the advantage of their higher decks as the ships grappled and the hand-to-hand fighting began. The advance of the Ottoman ships was slowed as many that had been struck by Venetian cannonballs began to wallow as the water rose in their holds, buying the Venetians a little precious time. On the Ottoman ships, a large number of Christian oarsmen had filed off their chains, and suddenly rose from their benches to attack the Egyptians with anything they could get their hands on. Mahomet Sirocco himself was killed, and his body, floating amid the tangle of ships, was picked up by the Venetians, beheaded, and his head displayed on a pike.

Among those Christians who had severed their fetters to rise up against the Turkish captors were convicts, debtors, thieves, bandits, assassins, gang members, and other unsavory sorts who had been sentenced to galley-oars instead of being kidnapped as so many others had been. Unlike the other Christian captives who sought to join in the fray, these men did not stick around for the worsening fighting, but as soon as they had got away from the Ottomans and had no immediate threat to prevent them doing so, they jumped overboard and swam for the Albanian shore, striking out into the mountains to resume their old lives of crime in a new country.

On Doria's side, the first contact with an Ottoman ship brought such an impetuous response from the European soldiers that they were able to seize Uchiali's ship in a single, determined rush aboard, Alessandro Farnese and his company of 200 among those storming the ship. Almost before the Turks could mount an opposition, the ship was in European hands. It was a giddy success for the Europeans, but hardly more than a first sally—the hard part still lay ahead. In order to block Uchiali's Algerian corsairs, Don Alvaro de Bazan brought in his reserves and engaged the long, irregular line of Ottoman ships, refusing to give a single oarsman or a meter of water. In the heat of this fighting, a Spanish artillery captain, his hand maimed by an Ottoman grenade and bleeding heavily, ordered one of his oarsmen to cut off his hand so he could bandage the stump and continue fighting. It is reported that the oarsman fainted, so the captain cut the hand off himself in order to carry on.

Uchiali and his old antagonist Giannandrea Doria were still locked in conflict, and Uchiali, who had beaten Doria once before, and badly, was planning to do it again, even though his ship was in European hands. Just as Mahomet Sirocco had attempted to run around the end of the Venetian line, so Uchiali tried much the same with the Genoese, forcing the two lines of ships nearer to the Morean shore. In spite of a courier in a *fregata* bringing word to Doria from Don Juan not to get too near the shore, Doria kept on his course, and in so doing, opened up a hole in the European line, a hole into which Uchiali ordered a half-dozen of his war galleys, and prepared to attack the Europeans from the rear.

At one time, as Doria's ships attempted to extend his line, the cry went up that the Genoese were flying—given Doria's clear reluctance for battle, not an entirely improbable development—and dismay spread through the European center, but a short time later a *fregata* carried word to Don Juan that Doria was still trying to keep from being outflanked by Uchiali's ships, that he had ordered his galleys to slip around Uchiali's flank, which accounted for his apparent flight, but that his ships were now firing on the enemy. This spread encouragement among the Europeans and gave many of the others the determination to carry on. The Genoese maneuvered along the Albanian shore, driving the Ottoman right back and into disarray.

As the lines began to break apart, clusters of fighting formed as small knots of ships tangled, grappled, and stormed decks as the battle became a matter of disputes over the control of decks. The pristine formations were lost in close-contested knots of war galleys and galliots. While cannon slammed at the waterlines of opposing ships, pistols, arquebuses, bows and arrows, and all manner of edged weapons were unleashed against the men in the ships. On the European ships, Christian oarsmen joined in the fighting with any weapon they could lay their hands on, sometimes taking chains from other oarsmen and using them like maces to bludgeon the Ottoman fighters. Rates of injury were very high, for men would not stop fighting unless incapacitated or killed.

By now, the air was thick with smoke, and it was becoming increasingly difficult for the two navies to maintain good observation of the battle's increasing confusion. Monks, assigned to chronicle the battle, were caught up in the excitement and laid about them with whatever came to hand. Some accounts say that Don Juan's pet marmoset joined in the fighting, picking up shells and arrows from the deck of the *Real* and dropping them into the sea; other accounts say that Uchiali had a pet hound that performed the same service. Given the steadily increasing chaos, such claims are hardly surprising, and unusual only for their ordinariness.

18

UCHIALI

B Y TWO IN the afternoon, the battle was going against the Turks all along their scattered line, in spite of their superior numbers, for the European engineering and technological improvements had provided sufficient advantage to offset the Ottoman volume of ships. There were drifting galleys on both sides, manned only by corpses, too damaged to be safely towed. In some instances, as the fighting became more dispersed, the numbers of clustered Ottoman vessels became unwieldy, and actually worked to the Ottoman disadvantage by creating the kind of congestion that prevented the Turks from positioning themselves well against the Europeans, so that they could not fire their cannon without endangering Ottoman ships as well as European ones. This was particularly critical on the Ottoman right, where many of their galleys were driven back into shallow water along the Albanian shore. The Europeans were able to close in on the disordered Ottoman ships and board them as they chose, taking prisoners and beating back soldiers before the Turks could rally a defensive line.

With most Ottoman commanders badly injured or dead, Uchiali became the rallying point of the Turks—at least for those who knew where he was. Aware that he stood to gain plunder and the Sultan's favor if he managed to turn the battle to Ottoman advantage, Uchiali was still enough of a corsair to maintain an every-man-for-himself posture, and left the slower ships to be stopped by the Genoese. In so doing, he decreased the number of his ships to a point that the Europeans had the advantage even while he strove to put distance between the main battle and his ships. Like Doria, Uchiali was not fond of pitched battles, preferring to cut, grapple, and run, getting treasure for himself with minor losses, and forcing his opponents to wear themselves out in fruitless pursuit of Uchiali's fast ships. But this was not a flight from battle, it was a rush toward it, and toward exacting a high price from the Europeans who had proved to be the most consistent thorn in the Ottomans' sides for the last two centuries.

Among the Ottoman military men, the Knights of Malta were the most loathed of Christian companies. Not only did the Knights operate as pirates in Ottoman waters, they were aggressively religious in a way that deeply offended Muslims, so that between their fighting prowess and their extremist variety of Christianity, they earned the bitterest enmity of the Turks. There were three Maltese galleys with Santa Cruz in the rearguard, and now that Uchiali was through Doria's line, he headed straight for *Capitana,* the Knights' flagship captained by Pietro Giustiniani, who was the sole survivor (but wounded five times with arrows and twice with blades) of those defending the ship. Thirty of his Knights and their men-at-arms died on the deck, for Uchiali was determined to seize the *Capitana,* which he took in tow after taking down the Maltese Cross banner of the Knights of Malta. With this much-prized trophy, Uchiali was prepared to call it a day.

Those Ottoman ships that had not broken through the European line faced a tricky position: the gulf is essentially a box-canyon, and although there was a long stretch of water behind the Ottoman ships, there was no escape from their position. Most of the Holy League ships were disinclined to give chase to the rear beyond getting the Turks to move out of firing range, but the Ottoman officers could not be certain that they would not be cornered at the rear, which prolonged the fighting along the Albanian shore, and ended in adding to Ottoman losses by about ten percent.

Meanwhile, with the Ottoman center now without leadership, and the ships hopelessly disarrayed, Don Juan de Austria was on a cursory cleanup of the center and the Turkish left on his way to relieve de Cardona, who was facing odds of two Ottoman galleys to every one of his squadron of Sicilian, Spanish, Papal, Tuscan, Savoyard, and Neapolitan galleys, daunting odds at any time, and particularly harsh in this quarterless battle. This engagement was one of the most bitterly fought of any at Lepanto, and it was bloody from the beginning to the end. The English seaman Thomas Hogg or Hodge, serving aboard a Neapolitan galley, reported many years later that "there were broken spars and shattered oars. . . . Galley-slaves were crushed between ships and left to hang in their chains. A man might walk across the water on the pieces of ships and men and not wet his feet. . . . Amid the broken wood were bodies, many of them oarsmen still fastened to their oars, and soldiers, their garments sodden with blood. It was as if the Last Trump had sounded and the sea was giving up its dead, not receiving more."

Uchiali's galleys that he had left behind were in the most grievous battle of their lives, and, being unable to escape, determined to take on the Europeans with all the fury they could muster. Exactly why the Ottoman galleys had to engage the Europeans is still open to debate, for there are conflicting explanations. One account, from a Jesuit among the Neapolitans, supposes that Uchiali had left the ships behind so that they could engage the enemy, thereby allowing Uchiali himself to escape, but others reporting from the round ships waiting with the European reserve stated that the ships in question had been damaged by cannon fire and were taking on water and therefore could not help but fall behind, and then be compelled to fight or face ignominious capitulation. Whatever the actuality was for Uchiali's rear ships, it meant that the Sicilians took the brunt of the attack from the Ottoman galleys lagging behind Uchiali's group. As a result, Don Juan de Cardona's squadron suffered the most devastating losses of any in the Holy League: on two ships, the Papal *San Giovanni* and one of the Savoyard galleys, every single officer and soldier either was killed in battle or died of his wounds afterward.

With that battle at its pitch, Uchiali, his prize *Capitana* in tow, was making for the Corinth Channel when Santa Cruz brought the rearguard into action again, this time to reclaim *Capitana,* for the Knights of Malta begrudged the Ottomans so much as a single oar from their ships. The galley *Guzman* pulled alongside *Capitana,* and two others pressed in on the opposite site of the corsair's ship, forcing Uchiali to cut the Maltese galley free in order to escape the converging Europeans. The only trophy Uchiali was able to take with him was the Knights' banner; he was followed by thirteen galleys and galliots, all bound for the protection of the Greek Islands. Had Uchiali remained to fight, it is doubtful the final results would have been much altered, but the degree of victory the Europeans enjoyed could have been considerably diminished by what Uchiali, with his corsair's tricks, might have accomplished. But since he decided to escape, the Ottomans, already in serious trouble, lost one of their craftiest commanders when he was most needed.

When the Venetian galley *Great Christ Risen Again* was boarded by Ottoman soldiers, her captain was killed in the main rush of Janissaries, and most of her officers fell soon after. With only the captain's secretary left to command the ship, the young man took a torch and set fire to the powder magazine, blowing himself and the ship to smithereens rather than allow it to fall into Ottoman hands. One of the *fregate,* carrying dispatches along the European left, was boxed in by four or five Ottoman galliots, and was deliberately sunk by her own crew to keep the dispatches she carried from the Ottomans. Other similarly heroic and desperate acts were recorded during the battle, many of which were accurate accounts of events, if somewhat exaggerated in tone.

With the Ottoman line broken and scattered, the last phase of the battle began, and what had begun as a jumble became a rout as the Turkish ships were surrounded and either sunk or grappled and towed by the Europeans. This ignominious end to what had seemed, only four hours earlier, a easy victory for the Ottomans was all the more distressing for the lack of resistance the Turks were able to muster once the Europeans took the lead in the battle. Now the challenge shouted to the Europeans to come and be slaughtered at the start of the fighting had a more than hollow ring. Those soldiers who surrendered now had to face the knowledge that they had lost their claims to any favor from the military or the Sultan, should they ever be granted release from European hands.

After the conclusion of the battle, Captain Ojeda of the *Guzman* reported that the thirty dead knights on the *Capitana* had killed over 300 Turks. Whether this was an overstatement or an accurate report, the Knights of Malta were satisfied with his account; they pensioned Ojeda for life in gratitude for his rescue of the *Capitana*.

19

INTERLUDES

A CCOUNTS ISSUED AFTER news of Lepanto spread throughout Europe described the scene at the Vatican on the morning of October 7, 1571, as being given over to discussions among the Pope and various financial officers of the Church on the costs of waging war against the Ottoman Empire—never mind it was Sunday. There had been no word from the European fleet for nearly a week, and Pius V was preparing to offer Mass for the Holy League later that day.

Suddenly, it was reported, the Pope broke off his conversation and went to the window where he stood looking up at the sky for several minutes, a rapt expression on his lean features. Then, his eyes filled with tears of joy, he told the Vatican treasurer that this was no time for anything but thanksgiving—that the Holy League was about to meet the Turks in battle, and that God would give them the victory. He claimed he had had a vision that the Holy League was under the care of Saint Michael and Saint George of Armenia, and that no foe could best them. He then went to the nearest chapel and fell on his knees before the crucifix. Word spread throughout the Vatican that the Pope had been granted a promise from Heaven of the triumph of the Holy League at the very moment the first shot was fired.

Less inspiring but also probably less apocryphal were Grand Vizier Sokolli's continuing efforts to conclude a separate peace with Venice, which continued right through the European naval campaign and the battle of Lepanto. With the help of the French—who had their own reasons for supporting the grand vizier's efforts—Sokolli did his utmost to break off the battle before it ever took place; he sent a private envoy to the Minor Consiglio who arrived in Venice on October 5 and was still in the city while Lepanto was being fought. The last thing that the grand vizier wanted was war with Venice, since that was bad for trade as well as potentially damaging for the Ottoman navy, to say nothing of the potential for the slaughter of Turks and Ottoman subjects held by Christians. Sokolli believed that the Ottoman military strength lay in their army, not their navy, and that putting their ships at risk had the potential of permanently damaging the Ottoman hold on Middle Eastern ports and the Greek Islands.

One of the points that the Sultan clung to was the rumor that the Ottomans possessed a second navy as vast as the one at Lepanto, and that at any time Selim could order those ships into battle against the Europeans, or that if it were necessary, another such navy could swiftly be built. There was no such navy, and there were no provisions to build one, but the Venetians—who did keep a large reserve of galleys—were willing to believe there might be, and therefore were inclined to discuss terms for a truce sooner than Sokolli expected. As eager as Selim was to continue to take on the Europeans, Sokolli finally persuaded him that there was more potential for harm than success. But by then Lepanto was over, and Sokolli's point had been proven beyond all debate.

20

BATTLE'S END

A S THE AUTUMN day began to fade, heavier and darker clouds gathered in the west—another omen for the Europeans, believed to be a sign that the might of a storm was supporting their cause. While the Holy League grappled those Ottoman ships that were salvageable, freed over 12,000 Christian galley slaves from those ships, and began to burn the wreckage that blundered among the remaining European ships, Don Juan set out on his tour of the ships that were still seaworthy. Half the European center was now joined with the right and the reserve containing those Ottoman ships that had not been able to escape to the rear or to break past the Holy League line with Uchiali, making toward the northwest and the Corinth Channel. A few other Ottoman war galleys were able to reach the protection of the harbor at Lepanto, but for the most part, the Turks surrendered or abandoned their ships as the Europeans took control of the site.

Giannandrea Doria's ship was undamaged—and was the only European flagship to have come through the battle unscathed—at the end of the day, and for all his pursuit of Uchiali, Doria had never actually exchanged cannon fire with him, although other Ottoman ships had fired on Doria's ship, and half the oars on the port side of the ship had been sheered off during close grappling with two Ottoman galleys. Doria greeted Don Juan aboard his ship awash with gore (but the blood was not his—one of his officers had been cut down by Ottoman cannon fire and bled all over him). More than many of the Europeans, Doria was prepared to loot the Ottoman ships as soon as Don Juan permitted the captains to board the Ottoman ships in order to seize treasure and ordnance left behind. Granting the captains this chance at pillage was common practice— even the Spanish, the Venetians, and the Pope had agreed upon shares of loot before undertaking the campaign—and for many seamen their only certain gain from the fight would be in the goods they claimed from the enemy ships.

On *Real,* one of the arquebusiers was revealed to be a woman, Maria the Dancer, who had come on the venture in order to stay with her lover, and who had acquitted herself with courage. She had killed at least one man on the *Sultana,* and for her valor was allowed to remain with her regiment and to have a share in the spoils allocated to the arquebusiers. So far as the official record goes, she was the only woman to have fought at Lepanto.

Many of the Ottoman galleys that had been driven back toward the Albanian shore had run aground, or had foundered and were listing on the beam-ends in shallow water, ready for the picking,; some were still grappled to their European counterparts, and the ships lay, half-sunk together, like the bodies of tragic lovers. Having been pounded by the fire from the galleasses, most of the Ottoman ships would never again be seaworthy, and their crews were too battered to mount any significant resistance to the arrival of the Europeans. But although there was good reason to fear the Holy League's seamen, the first order of business was gathering those European dead who could be found.

As the fighting wound down, on some of the Ottoman ships still afloat the remaining soldiers were running out of cannonballs, and so threw whatever they could lay their hands on at the Europeans, including oranges and lemons, which brought about a great deal of laughter from the exhausted Europeans, and for which the remaining

Ottoman soldiers were chagrined. Even Ottoman galley slaves rallied
to hold off the Europeans for fear that they were so intoxicated with
slaughter that they would kill the oarsmen before thinking of liberat-
ing them.

Astonished by their triumph, European galleys still able to move
easily went about the stretch of water they had fought so relentlessly
to control; in the fading light they did their utmost to determine
their losses as measured against the Ottomans', taking stock of the
wreckage of the Ottoman navy, securing the Ottoman ships still
afloat, boarding those safe enough to be looted, and attempting to
identify and record the dead and dying from both sides. Gradually
lanterns were lit, and eerie platforms of luminance slid over the car-
nage in the water, removing barrels and weapons and bodies from
among the ruined ships, shattered oars, and the gory detritus of battle. Their jubilation was measured against the stunning loss of 7,600
European dead and as many wounded; the cost for their triumph had
been shockingly high, and had numbered among its toll some of the
most well-reputed officers in the major fighting forces of Europe.

21

FIRST RECKONING

IN THE FIRST two days following Lepanto, estimates of deaths among the Ottomans ran as high as 30,000 men; over 3,000 were taken prisoner. Between 15,000 and 16,000 Christian galley slaves were liberated, roughly 2,500 of whom were Spaniards, some of whom had been chained to the same bench and oar for more than four years (both Europeans and Ottomans considered six years to be the longest possible life for an oarsman once he was chained in position). More than 12,000 Ottoman soldiers were secured to European oars. Almost three-quarters of the Ottoman navy—some 240 galleys and galliots—was sunk, wrecked, burned, or captured, losses the Sultan could not readily sustain, no matter how he might boast that he could launch another such fleet with keels of gold and anchor-chains of silver.

The Ottomans also had more than 300 of their cannon captured in usable condition, although many other guns were lost to both sides during the battle when the galleys collided or listed. The light galliots had smaller and fewer cannon and provided less of a prize in that regard than their war galleys did. The ponderous galleasses, carrying about eighty cannon apiece, had the fewest losses—their very size kept them from being boarded and their firepower held the Ottomans at too great a distance to sink them.

Despite both sides' claims for significantly higher numbers, it is likely that between 50,000 and 55,000 men fought for the Europeans,

while 60,000 to 67,000 men were on the Ottoman side—high numbers for that period in history even without the usual enlargement of
numbers. The European deaths were probably between 7,000 and
9,000 men, about half of whom were Venetian. The Holy League lost
twelve war galleys from their main squadrons and another three from
their reserves, and salvaged over fifty cannon from damaged European
ships. These are substantial losses, but not nearly as devastating as the
amounts among the Ottomans, nor did they have as far-reaching ram-
ifications: as of that Sunday evening, the superiority of Ottoman sea
power had ended, and would not be restored.

Shortly after sunset, a Roman Capuchin monk reported in his official journal seeing two Ottoman scout ships darting out from the
cover of a wallowing, rudderless Turkish galley, bound to the southeast, away from the European ships. No pursuit was made, for the
scout ships had nowhere to go but the closed end of the gulf. It might
have been that the scout ships carried officers or treasures that they
intended to put ashore as far from the European ships as possible, but
that is nothing more than conjecture; no other account of fleeing
scout ships was made by anyone keeping accounts for the Holy
League at the time, so the Roman Capuchin may have seen only drifting wreckage and mistaken it for moving ships. Aside from this report, after the battle was over, no Ottoman ship was observed to get
away from the Europeans. It is remarkable that there were no more
such reports, for only in a wholly decisive victory would that be the
case—usually in naval battles of the period, many ships were said to
have got away by luck, guile, or stealth, all of which had forsaken the
Ottomans at Lepanto.

An hour after sunset the wind whipped up and it began to rain,
slowing the rescue and looting efforts, and turning a chilly day un-
pleasantly cold. The various soldiers and sailors occupied with pulling
the dead from the water in order to identify them left off their work
and sought shelter below-decks, determined to ride out the storm

without risking being swept overboard—a very real possibility. A few men retrieving barrels and other flotsam tied themselves to the deck-rail in order to continue to troll for valuables, but as the storm worsened, even they abandoned their endeavors and retreated to the protection of the holds, where many of them were put to work making repairs in the hulls, caring for the wounded, and making inventories of equipment, weapons, ordnance, medicines, and food. Scouts were posted to keep watch on the port of Lepanto in case the Ottomans tried something desperate, but they remained inside the fortress, the gun emplacements conspicuously manned.

Morning was not much improved: the rain continued although the wind slacked off. The ships were not able to move very far, not just because of the weather, but due as well to the need for careful inspection to check all the ships for damage, leaking, waterlogging, then for numbers of injured and dead aboard, bodies and parts of bodies still floating in the water around the ships, general readiness, and the need to determine which men—particularly former Ottoman oarsmen—were able to sail the ships back toward Europe. These tasks were as necessary as they were tedious, and the men undertaking the inspections were often met with annoyance and disdain from comrades preferring to bask in the glow of victory than to spend time poking about the holds and bilges, looking for damage. In addition, the re-supply ships had been delayed, or had not yet been reached by the *fre-gate* sent out to find them, and as a result the Europeans were without much-needed foodstuffs and medical supplies, so that even as the storm slacked off, there was no improvement of the Europeans' immediate circumstances.

About all that Monday offered was a greater opportunity to loot: *Sultana* provided extensive gilding on its raised poop deck, and a hoard of sequins (gold Turkish coins) in chests in the hold; another trove of sequins was found in the corsair Kara Hodja's hold, along with all manner of loot from a year's worth of piracy. Even small chests of sea-bread, sacks of beans and lentils, lengths of cloth, and occasional barrels of salt-beef were taken aboard the European ships, to be divided promptly by the men—not always along strict lines of fairness or need. The meals prepared were not festive—they were not fancy or lavish enough—they were to alleviate hunger, cold, and exhaustion, and were little more than the essential minimum the men required, since, without storming the harbor-fortress of Lepanto and taking whatever the Ottomans had left, the Europeans would have to make do with their dwindling supplies, at least, it was assumed, for a few more days. And, thanks to the capture of so many oarsmen (now liberated) and seamen, they had more men to feed.

Problems arose as some of the injured became ill due to lack of medical attention—admittedly not very effective in those days even under the best of circumstances—and had to be looked after by increasingly large numbers of seamen. Some of the wounded were Turkish captives, their condition demanding attention only because of the potential of spreading sickness and the possible loss of ransom if the prisoner should die. Meals continued Spartan in their simplicity, and water had to be rationed, even with the rain keeping most of the crews under cover. The oarsmen on the outriggers had awnings spread above them, but they did little to keep out the wet; soon the captains began to worry about the possibility of illness breaking out among the oarsmen, which could strand them there in what might still be Ottoman waters.

Without the delivery of food to sustain them, and with a few Ottoman ships back under the protection of the Lepanto guns, the leaders of the European fleet decided to leave the gulf before the Ottomans could dispatch another navy from Constantinople—which many feared they would do—and headed out the Corinth Channel on the ninth of October, leaving the fortress of Lepanto itself untouched. A number of Europeans had wanted to storm its battlements, raze the walls, and carry off more loot, a dispute that became quite heated, especially among the volunteers who depended upon plunder for their pay. But with the weather in danger of turning stormy again, and sailing increasingly dangerous, Don Juan decided that they should begin their voyage home while they still had some hope of reaching their home ports before winter weather stopped them at the nearest safe harbor they could find and kept them isolated.

It was still assumed that the Sultan had a second navy as vast as the one the Europeans had just defeated, a navy that the Europeans would be unable to crush as it had the galleys that came out from Lepanto, and that as soon as news of the Ottoman defeat reached other flotillas, there would be a convergence of Ottoman ships on the European ships. In that event, it was understood the Holy League might not fare as well against them, so moving out beyond the Gulf of Patmas—which would, by spring, be known as the Gulf of Lepanto, at least to Europeans—and the Corinth Channel was essential, and that could not begin until the basic distribution of the loot and captives had been accomplished to the satisfaction of all the officers, a process that became more complex with every passing hour. The preparedness of this mythic second navy became more formidable with every telling of its might and every passing hour its legend was repeated. By the late afternoon, the Europeans were well on their way to scaring themselves off the seas, and so distracted themselves from plundering the last of the Ottoman ships.

Before dealing with the accumulated spoils could turn into the excuse for hostilities among the Europeans, Marcantonio Colonna came up with guidelines for handling disputes in that regard, and most of the acrimony was avoided. To further ameliorate the situation, as well as to endear himself to his seamen and soldiers, Don Juan, entitled to ten percent of all recovered loot, gave his share to the wounded men because they had been unable to pursue gaining treasure for themselves; he did not want them to be deprived because they were injured. Later, when he was awarded a gift of 30,000 ducats by the city of Messina when the fleet returned there, Don Juan gave it to the wounded men as well, gaining their devotion from that time on.

While waiting for the supply ships to arrive, Don Juan made his official report that would be given to the *fregata* accompanying the supply ships returning to Messina, where it would be passed to couriers to be taken to Felipe II. It was so diplomatic that Marcantonio Colonna might well have written it, for the report scarcely mentions the wound Don Juan received ("a scratch I hardly notice") or the degree of damage inflicted on his ship ("the *Real* sustained no serious impairment beyond the breaking of her oars"). He was generous with his praise for the oarsmen, the soldiers—in particular the volunteers—and the seamen who strove so mightily to stay the course of the battle.

Amid his many items of praise, he made no real complaint of Doria's circumspection, since the Genoese commander was Felipe's own man, and represented Felipe's view of their military potential. Once he had accorded his good opinion to his senior officers, he asked for consideration to many of his lesser officers, especially those who, like himself, were bastards, and therefore not officially allowed to participate in the division of plunder. He reiterated his high praise for the oarsmen with some force, and repeated his indebtedness to the volunteer soldiers, without whom he stated the battle would not have gone half so well, as if he was worried that Felipe might not be willing to accord the degree of recognition to these men that they had earned; he also gave credit to the Ottomans for putting so many fine seamen and soldiers on the line. He took no credit for the victory for himself, thanking God for saving them all in the fight. To make the report more welcome, he included the green silk Mecca prayer banner, taken from *Sultana,* as a personal trophy of the battle. He also arranged for Sultan Selim's imperial banner to be carried to Pope Pius V. Both gestures would stand him in good stead later on.

By the time the first few reports had made it back to western Europe, anxiety had reached a dreadful high, and the rumors circulating had taken on momentous proportions. Under such heightened apprehension, the reality of the battle—good, bad, or indifferent—was embraced with an avidity that fed all manner of hysteria before any official accounts were announced. In some cases, court gossip had already decided who was a hero and who was not for no reason other than to appear to know something about what was happening, so the political significance of the various participants was assigned for many of the officers long before their actual behavior was reported, in the name of supporting the Holy League.

For the most part, the perceptions were fairly uniform, but not always. Upon hearing of Doria's lack of zeal, the Pope, unlike Felipe, was not best-pleased, and hinted broadly that the Genoese commander would do well to maintain his vaunted prudence by avoiding Rome for the next few years, advice Doria was more than willing to take, for Papal disapproval would take away from the current haze of glory that enveloped him.

When the Holy League ships finally arrived at Corfu, on October 24, they found the supply ships waiting, their captains unwilling to set out in foul weather for fear of losing the items they carried to inclement seas as well as risking frostbite for the oarsmen. Instead of wandering about uncertainly, calling at ports that might be in enemy hands, the European supply ships had decided to remain in the most likely place, and let the Holy League come to them. That most of the captains in the flotilla agreed with this determination drove Don Juan almost to the point of rebuking them, but he knew that would only serve to alienate the very men whose help he most needed, so he confined his complaint to a note to Don Garcia de Toledo.

Waiting for the Holy League ships to find them was the sort of decision that might be expected from officers answering to Felipe II, and had the Holy League not found them when they did would have compelled the European heroes to raid the coasts for sustenance, much like any Ottoman corsair or war galley, for they were down to half-rations at a time when much more was needed.

With the safe arrival of the Holy League ships, the island gave itself up to feasting and celebration for three days, marking each evening with a display of fireworks and lavish fetes, already enlarging upon the heroic deeds of the Europeans against the Ottomans. By the time the festivities were over, the ghastly reality of battle had begun to be suffused with the poetic vision of those who had not endured the reality but who were prepared to bask in the remarkable achievement. Songs and ponderous verse were made to commemorate the victory—gestures that would continue for some time to come. Lepanto was well on its way to entering the realms of myth well before it was a recognized actuality. Reputations were made, lost, and enhanced as the tales of Lepanto began to spread throughout the European ports, eventually reaching out from there, along the trade routes from the New World to the farthest reaches of the Baltic Sea, the Atlantic, and the Indian Oceans.

22

DEVELOPMENTS

THE EUROPEANS DID not make a completely clean sweep of the Ottoman ships without incurring some losses to themselves—for the next several months requests came in for ransoms for Europeans taken captive during the battle. Even the Pope had to ransom his nephew, Paolo Ghislieri, who, upon his return to Rome was exiled for repeated misdemeanors. One of the captured Turkish officers offered his services to the Spanish crown as an intelligence operative and, apparently, was accepted, for he was welcomed at the Escorial by two of Felipe's ministers, but he was not mentioned in any documents again beyond the initial one, not even as a prisoner or hostage.

The English pirate Sir Thomas Stukeley improved his reputation and took to privateering (piracy, but with a royal license to prey upon England's enemies so long as he split the loot with the queen) until his role in the plot to restore Catholicism to England was uncovered, at which time he returned to the Continent and a military life. One of the French volunteers managed to gain four full shares of loot through gambling, and was able to restore his family's fortunes upon his return home, marry well, and become a minor noble before he died twenty years later.

An Ottoman scout ship, blown off course while making its way around the end of the Peloponnese, bound for Constantinople, ended up being half-wrecked on Hydros, and, according to local legend, its small crew was rescued by the Brothers of Saint Spiridion, whose monastery overlooked the shore where the scout ship wrecked. Taken to the monastery to be nursed, the Ottoman seamen determined to kill the monks once they were healthy enough to continue their voyage. But by the time they had recovered, they were also converted, and became the next generation of monks at the monastery. Although this tale smacks of pious fiction, it does appear that an Ottoman ship was wrecked there in the winter of 1571–72, so there may be a note of truth in it.

Not all the results were ultimately beneficial for the veterans of either side. A surviving Sardinian armorer was granted a house and land for his bravery, which he lost in a spate of dicing three years after he was rewarded with them. At a hearing to determine the legality of the transfer, the veteran protested the loss of his reward for his achievement at Lepanto, to which the magistrate hearing the case remarked, "A veteran of such a battle should know better than to throw away his prize." A Scottish volunteer, upon returning home with enough money to buy a dozen sheep, was excoriated publicly for supporting the Catholic Church, which the good Protestant divine in his town thought to be an immoral and corrupt institution; the Scottish volunteer was forced to relocate his sheep and his family to another village. A Flemish arquebusier set up a dockside tavern near Bruges where he helped kidnap unwary sailors to work aboard merchant ships, turning to his advantage the contacts he had made at Lepanto; this was a highly illegal activity, for which he was apprehended and hanged.

A steersman from one of Uchiali's abandoned ships was taken captive by the Europeans and carried back to Messina where he was assigned to an oar on a Spanish Holy League galley. He labored there for two years, his family being unwilling or unable to ransom him; the galley ran aground near Tunis, where the steersman escaped with most of the oarsmen and headed for Tunis. He was captured not far from the city by slavers, and was castrated before being sent with a train of slaves and slave dealers to Egypt, where he died in the service of a Mameluke noble, six years later, and was given a funeral procession and a mural inscription at the local mosque by the noble because of his participation in Lepanto, which the noble regarded as a pious act.

In Sicily, a goldsmith—or perhaps brother goldsmiths—named Giorgio and/or Gregorio Maestrobiaggio developed a new, faster, and more efficient process for removing gold leaf from metal and wood. He—or they—purchased decorative sections of gilt taken from Turkish ships by the Holy League seamen and soldiers as they returned to Messina and, while paying a fair price for the gilded objects, because of his—or their—improved process netted a tidy fortune in less than a year. Several of the armorers with the Holy League fleet laid claim to as many Ottoman weapons as possible during the post-battle looting. Those items they could not use as recovered they melted down and recast for later sale, and some they offered to European nobles as souvenirs of the battle. They also took objects of personal adornment with the expectation of selling them privately in Europe.

A few outcomes were deeply satisfactory: Maria the Dancer was officially enrolled in her regiment and was paid the same amount as the men who fought at Lepanto. Prospero Colonna, Marcantonio's heir, gained favorable recognition for his role in the battle, which, while it did not have much impact on the illustrious Colonna family in general, did gain the young man more rapid advancement and more distinction than would have been the case otherwise, earning a trust that he fulfilled admirably. And a Spanish soldier named Miguel Cervantes headed for home with a maimed hand and a changed view of chivalry.

It took time for official word of the victory to be carried from Greece to Europe, and for some while the success of the European venture was generally unknown. The Venetians, many of whom were set to building fortifications and protective earthworks for their city, were alarmed when, on October 17, a Venetian war galley came in sight manned by turbaned sailors. Fearing the worst, they prepared to repel the ship when they heard the shouts from the war galley that the sailors were Venetians, and their turbans were trophies—a fine way of demonstrating their victory. They displayed the Turkish banners that trailed in the sea from their afterdeck, a sign that the Ottomans were vanquished.

On the Venetian islands anxiety turned to rejoicing, and the war galley was welcomed with the clamor of Venetian churchbells and the report of pistol fire. People boiled out to the waterfront to see the war galley arrive and to give it a proper welcome. There was shouting and singing and giddy celebration. When the war galley actually tied up and the men disembarked, they were swarmed upon by the grateful, giddy populace. The Venetians sent off news to all the significant members of the Holy League, their notices arriving sometimes many days in advance of the official dispatches from Don Juan and his officers, and stealing a little of the thunder of the actual commanders.

The next day there was a Te Deum at the Basilica of Saint Mark, and a public day of celebration was declared. Just as well, for the city was caught up in jubilation, and all manner of impromptu festivities had begun from the docks to the gaming houses, to the churches, to the brothels, and, without some form of direction might have turned into more riot than elation. The Minor and Maggior Consiglii made declarations of thanks to the Venetians who had fought the Turks, and added thanks to the other Europeans as an afterthought. Official declarations from the Doge to Felipe and the Pope were dispatched along with congratulatory gifts. But although Venice stood to do more damage to the Ottoman maritime empire, in the end they did not, apparently preferring peace and trade to war. Whatever the final reason was for this decision, Venetian territory was not attacked by any Ottoman force for the next sixty-eight years, although the corsairs continued their cut-and-run piracy in the eastern Mediterranean, occasionally stalking the larger flotillas from Europe, of the faster, larger Brenton (*bertoni*) ships from the English Channel, but preferentially taking their prey from smaller round-ship merchant fleets, for it was realized that no matter what posturing the Sultan might indulge in, he would not risk ships he did not have against a navy that had beaten him so badly.

Don Garcia de Toledo, who had taught Don Juan a great deal about naval strategy, was so delighted to hear of the victory that he began to conjure up plans for the conquest of Jerusalem, even though he knew it could not happen; diplomatic reality and complex national interests made it inexpedient for more aggressive actions to be taken against the Ottoman Empire, particularly since none of the governments associated with the Holy League could reach a compromise on their goals. Gamely, Don Garcia made an attempt to convince Don Juan to tackle the mission, saying "Heaven has made you its favorite" by way of persuasion, but he was not surprised or even disappointed when Don Juan politely declined the proposition: Don Garcia would not want to tarnish the current shine of military glory that Don Juan enjoyed, and such a risky venture as retaking Jerusalem might very well do just that. Don Garcia made another suggestion—that the Ottoman capital be taken instead. With Constantinople once again in Christian hands, the Turks would have to turn their attention elsewhere, such as toward Ukraine and Russia.

His enthusiasm reflected a growing ambition among the European powers—with the exception of Venice—who wanted to send the Holy League off to conquer Constantinople itself, although none of the governments seemed willing to pay for another naval expedition such as the one that had just been fought; the cost would be staggering, and if the expedition should fail, all that was accomplished at Lepanto would be lost. The more the risks were considered, the more overwhelming they appeared until the potential advantages of such an action shrank to almost nothing, and the risks assumed enormous proportions.

As the spring came on and no new naval push came from the Turks, the Europeans breathed a collective sigh of relief, and their exuberance shifted away from naval adventurism to market expansion, something that would shore up instead of further empty civic coffers. Public sentiment was running high, however, and many Lepanto veterans found themselves chastised by those same people who had praised them while the flush of success was upon them, complaining at the Holy League's failure to bring down the Sultan as well as his navy by going on to Constantinople and sacking the city—convictions still shared by Don Garcia and a number of experienced military men, and argued on many occasions for the next thirty years.

23

REACTIONS SPREAD

O N HIS OFFICIAL announcement of the triumph at Lepanto in Rome, Pope Pius declared *"Fuit homo missus a Deo, cui nomen erat Joannes."* There was a man sent out for God, whose name was John; meaning that full credit for the victory was given to Don Juan de Austria, which, while a simplistic assignment of credit that could be readily grasped by the public, created a potential for rancor among the other commanders, and was not the way to guarantee the continuing support for the Holy League from Felipe II. The Pope's enthusiastic and wholehearted praise—heartily endorsed in Rome—created a climate of disapproval of Don Juan in Spain, who was seen to be ambitious; it was a perception that, thanks to envious whispers at court, never entirely lifted.

As the fleet made its way home, all of Europe welcomed the men who fought at Lepanto, in many instances conferring honors where none were deserved, or lauding the tall tales of the fight rather than the battle as it was. Lepanto had stirred European self-respect, and those who had been against taking the Turks on ever, in any form, now became confident of European superior seamanship and maritime strength. Along with the social reforms of the Reformation, there now was a more expansive vision of the European place in the world. Between Spanish expansion in the New World and this defeat of the Ottoman navy, Europeans began to reassess themselves, to move toward a much broader participation beyond their own countries, and with greater goals than trade or conquest to motivate them—the great age of exploration was underway.

More and greater rejoicing followed in Rome, until, on a cold, sunny December 4, 1571, the portly, dignified Marcantonio Colonna, in his finest array, including the Order of the Golden Fleece hanging on his breast, capped all previous festivities when he entered the city on a white jennet leading 120 Turkish prisoners, chained in pairs, a deliberate harkening back to the triumphal processions of the Caesars. Rome went joyously berserk, with dancing in the streets and patriotic displays. Given Pius' austerity, no official banquet was offered at the Vatican, but a generous donation was made to provide dowries for charity girls as an indication of thanksgiving for the victory. No matter: many of the city's most eminent families—the Colonne first among them—took up the slack left by the Pope in the matter of parties, feasts, and processions of patriotic delight. The Pope might shun any hint of decadence, but the Romans still knew how to party, and with so splendid an excuse as this, threw themselves into it with verve and magnificence.

Matters in Genoa, although celebratory, were a long way from the near-saturnalia of delectation that had filled Rome, or the frenzied merrymaking in Venice: a few select civic banquets, a presentation of honors to a few of the officers, a religious procession, and a donation to the city's hospitals was about as much as Genoa was willing to do. It was not simply because there had been questions asked about Giannandrea Doria's conduct at Lepanto, but the doubts he created concerning his own record were such that Genoa faced a degree of embarrassment for its policy of being unwilling to risk ships on campaign; in so conclusive a battle, hesitation was tantamount to poltroonism. Also, as Spanish territory, anything too outlandish by way of festivities would earn the sere disapproval of Felipe II, which no one wanted. So the government deliberately praised Doria for the care he took of the Genoese and Spanish ships, and his high concern for the safety of his men, but at the same time, they did not precisely heap Doria with honors and awards for what he had done. Tacitly it was understood that many in Genoa had expected the Europeans not to fight, and if they fought, not to win.

Among the many who had not expected the Europeans to win, there was a constant and sinister reminder that there could well be another campaign, and that it might not go as well as the Lepanto venture had—the rumor of the second Ottoman navy had been heard in Rome as well as Venice—and with that as a factor, many believed that a second clash with the Turks would end less happily than this one had. A great number of second-guessers were starting to antici-pate what they could expect from the Ottomans, and the Church paid a great deal of attention to the distresses being bruited about Rome. Many of the high-ranking churchmen managed to be thrilled and apprehensive at once, delighted that the Sultan had suffered so unexpected a setback even while fearing the vengeance they believed would be unleashed upon them, lending their merriment an edginess that had not been part of the celebrations in Venice.

Not surprisingly, Felipe II's response was more restrained than the Pope's. His notification from Venice arrived while he was attending Vespers, and he did not allow the service to be interrupted, for that was too indecorous for the straightlaced Felipe. Only when Vespers was over did the King of Spain announce the good news of the Lepanto victory to the congregation and order a Te Deum sung. Every year thereafter a Mass has been said in Toledo cathedral to commemorate the Lepanto victory, for which Felipe gave sole and entire credit to God, although he did allow Don Juan's battle pennant to be hung there once Don Juan returned to Spain. In an uncharacteristic burst of praise, in his letter to Don Juan, Felipe told his half-brother that he was "happy to learn of your excellent conduct in the fighting, for it is most gratifying that one of mine has been permitted to prosecute this great work for the glory of our faith."

But Felipe could not remain positive about the victory, not when there were still Ottoman galleys and corsairs to contend with, and he complained to the Papal Nuncio and three of his advisors that Don Juan had been willing to endanger many ships and Christian lives, yet through God's Grace, and God's Grace alone, had attained the goal, but that he might just as well have lost all in taking such chances. Pleased though Felipe was to have the Ottoman navy driven from the sea, leaving the Spanish Empire undoubted master of all the seas and oceans, he seemed incapable of expressing any untainted approval of what his bastard half-brother had accomplished, or of admitting that Lepanto had truly benefited Spain more than any other European country.

Perhaps it was his sense of propriety that prevented Felipe's extending any bonhomie to Don Juan, perhaps it was his jealousy at the admiration Don Juan had had heaped upon him, and perhaps he believed the courtiers who whispered that Don Juan was set upon using his military success to advance himself politically, and at Felipe's expense. Whatever the underlying reason, the Lepanto triumph only served to drive the wedge more deeply between Don Juan and Felipe, and as a result, Felipe soon found an excuse to remove Don Juan from his court, sending him back to sea with a mandate to finish what he had begun, and keeping him with the Holy League navy in Sicily, away from the Spanish court.

24

IN CONSTANTINOPLE

MAKING A CIRCUITOUS return through the Greek Islands to Constantinople, Uchiali reverted to his corsair habits and picked off a single Venetian galley, somewhat damaged and lagging in the rear behind the Holy League. Using this one vessel as a sop for the Sultan, and as a way to lessen the chance that he might be blamed for the ruin of the fleet, Uchiali took it in tow and made for home through the various channels among the Greek Islands, afraid that he might be followed by the Venetians, and determined to elude them. The news he brought to the Sultan he knew would not be welcome: all the other top-rank officers at Lepanto were wounded or dead and the fleet was destroyed. The only trophy that the Sultan could display was the ensign of the Knights of Malta's *Capitana*, which was hung in the principal mosque of Constantinople, which had once been the Church of the Most Holy Wisdom (Hagia Sophia).

With the virtual elimination of the senior naval officers, the Ottoman marine military was in disarray, and in spite of his elevation to hero, Uchiali was in no position to help reestablish the navy. As a corsair, he pursued a very different kind of seagoing strategy than that needed to restore the fleet to fighting significance. This left the decisions in the hands of courtiers and army officers, all of whom had better uses for the money and Janissaries that had been allocated to the navy. Uchiali could not even advise the Divan as to the number of ships needed to take on the Europeans again, or recommend changes in ship design to counter the improvements in the Venetian war galleys and galleasses. Such matters were outside of his concerns, and he regarded them as insignificant when compared to captured slaves and treasure.

Aside from the frenzy of shipbuilding that took over many parts of the city—including parts of the Imperial Gardens—the Constantinopolitans began improved fortifications on the city walls, but soon abandoned them as the costs soared and the Sultan's court took to bickering about what part of the city was most at risk. About all they could agree upon were the main docks, and too much military reinforcement would interfere with trade, which no one wanted. But something needed to happen—that much was obvious to everyone.

Once the degree and scope of the defeat at Lepanto had been realized by Selim, the Sultan gave vent to his awesome temper, demanding that every Spaniard and Venetian—although some reports are more comprehensive and say every Christian—in Constantinople be arrested and executed within the next two days. Fortunately Sokolli and the moderates managed to dissuade Selim from this slaughter, suggesting that now was not the time to goad the Europeans, not if any sort of normal relations were to be restored. In addition, the French ambassador, still trying to work something out between the Ottomans and the Venetians, made it clear that the Venetians would refuse to treat with anyone responsible for the murder of 40.000 of their coreligionists. It is to Sokolli's credit that he was able to rein in his excitable Sultan by reminding Selim that there were thousands of Ottomans living in Christian countries, and if the Turks killed Christians, the Christians might do the same to the Turks. When some more hawkish members of the Divan opined that Christians might not have the strength of character for so much killing, Sokolli reminded them: "We said as much before Lepanto, and we erred." This appears to have been the most convincing argument, for no more suggestions of wholesale murder were put forth.

Through much of the winter, Constantinople built war galleys, and by the following May had completed 150 ships. They were light war galleys, similar to the fast, responsive ships of the corsairs, but as a result, could not carry heavy guns in quantity. To make matters worse, the wood from which they were built was unseasoned, and tended to warp after a few months at sea, requiring immediate and extensive repairs. The cannon, too, had problems, for since they had been hastily cast there were tiny flaws in the metal; as a result, they would occasionally explode rather than fire, particularly when allowed to get too hot through repeated firing. This was not only extremely hazardous to the Ottoman gunners and ships, it tended to make the sailors chary of handling the cannon, or of working anywhere near them. Suggestions that European cannon might be purchased were met with ire—who could trust the Europeans to sell the Turks proper cannon? In matters of other arms, the Sultan was a bit more flexible: with the support of Selim himself, Uchiali purchased 20,000 arquebuses for his marine soldiers, bought one hundred bales of heavy canvas for sails, ordered the capture of Morean Greek youths and strong Basran herders from the Persian Gulf to man the oars of the new ships. The canvas of the sails was from France, and other European merchants provided hemp, lumber, tackle, and brass.

Although Sokolli was on his way to becoming the most powerful grand vizier in history, he did not gain everything he sought. He had to support and endorse the absurd triumph that Selim insisted on giving Uchiali. To see his oldest rival, of all people, held up as a hero must have irked Sokolli tremendously. Nonetheless, he went along, as much to keep the war in diplomatic hands and uninfluenced by eager military commanders as to indulge Selim. When Uchiali was made Admiral of the Fleet, Sokolli did not oppose it; it may be that he realized the advancement was more show than content, for the few ships actually remaining in the fleet were not intended to venture beyond Constantinople: the object was to have impressive ships for foreigners to see, but not endanger them by taking them into battle. Unlike Uchiali and the Sultan, Sokolli had learned his lesson.

Orthodox Christians, while offering prayers of thanksgiving for the Holy League's victory in their churches, were restrained in their celebrations, for although they knew that the Ottoman navy was well and truly overcome, they realized that they could be accused of sedition for spreading information about the European triumph, and they were aware that many of the Sultan's court were searching for some way to punish Christians for the defeat of their navy. That was one of the reasons that news of Lepanto tended to move slowly through the Orthodox branch of Christianity—that, and for six weeks or so, Christians were restricted to their districts by order of Grand Vizier Sokolli, who was afraid of anti-Christian riots and military forcible drafting of young Christian men, both of which were very real possibilities.

When Selim met with his military leaders during the winter, it was agreed that attacks on Europeans would take place overland, through regions they had already conquered—such as Bosnia and Hungary—and would strike at important cities away from the coasts, in Poland, Slovakia, Bohemia, Bavaria, and Austria; eventually Ottoman forces would retake Spain, and then claim France and Italy. Selim had got it into his head that most important European cities were inland, on rivers, not on the coasts, and so wasting time and effort by coastal attacks was a poor use of soldiers and weapons. But he kept up the shipbuilding, as much to demonstrate the Ottoman capability to restore the navy as from any inclination to use it. Most of the territory Selim had his eyes on was held by the Austrian branch of the Hapsburgs, and was caught up in the turmoil of the Reformation, a social upheaval almost totally misunderstood by the Ottomans, and therefore badly misjudged in its significance.

To exacerbate matters, a combination of sharp inflation and regional uprisings took a toll on the Ottoman economy, forcing a devaluation of coinage that was of short-term benefit but ultimately disastrous, for it damaged trade and compromised Ottoman reliability from Spain to the Persian Gulf. Ottoman coins became so debased that they were called leaves for their lightness. Through the next five years, the commercial might of the Ottoman Empire was eroded beyond repair, and although there was some improvement a century and a half later, the flow of wealth was inexorably changed, leaving the Ottoman Empire to steady depletion of riches and property.

The Ottoman dependence on slaves increased during the time the value of their money decreased, and that made for precarious relations with some of their buffer states, for it was from these regions that most of the new slaves were taken; semi-autonomous regions actively resisted complying with increased Ottoman demands for slaves. Add to that a stepped-up compulsory draft, and it is easy to see why regional corruption took a sharp upswing during the next four decades, and why regional politics became much nastier than they had been, for bribery became the only way to avoid open brush-fire wars—and bribery came in many forms.

Sokolli did manage to achieve one of his major goals and conclude a separate peace with Venice in the spring of 1573. For the losing side, Sokolli got excellent terms for the Ottomans: Venice regained her trading privileges and her access to ports, but all Venetian prisoners had to be ransomed, while Turkish prisoners in Venice were to be released without any payment. Promising to protect Venice against Spanish incursion, Sokolli insisted that Venice could launch only sixty new galleys per year as compared to 300 permitted to the Sultan's navy, and Venice had to pay reparation in the sum of 300,000 sequins. Had the Sultan actually followed through with ships, this treaty might have given him a second crack at European sea power, but that was not to happen.

After Lepanto, no one in Turkey wanted to become engaged in naval confrontations, and the new policy quickly shifted the emphasis away from the Mediterranean and toward eastern Europe through Bulgaria, Romania, Hungary, Serbia, Bosnia, and on toward Austria, Bohemia, and southern Poland. For the next century, Ottoman aggression in Europe would run along these corridors until finally being stopped at the walls of Vienna in September, 1683. In the decades following Vienna, the Ottoman presence in eastern Europe would steadily diminish and retreat until the end of the nineteenth century, when it took its last gasps in the troubled decade prior to World War I.

Yet is it interesting to note that today, alone among the Middle Eastern countries, Turkey—the successor to the Ottoman Sultanate— has succeeded in creating and maintaining a secular Islamic society. Perhaps the hard years following Lepanto showed the hazards of theocratic government more clearly than anyone assumed at the time. It certainly exacted a high price from the Ottoman people, one that remained with them well into the eighteenth century.

25

MORE REPERCUSSIONS

RONICALLY, ALTHOUGH LEPANTO demonstrated the full potential of galley warfare, it was the last major battle of galley fleets ever fought. Soon after, improvements in sail design and adaptation of ship construction for long ocean voyages shifted dependance to galleons, which did not rely on oarsmen, were more maneuverable than even galliots were, and had the additional advantage of needing much smaller complements of seamen to sail, since they required no oarsmen to be accommodated either at their oars or in terms of upkeep. As the Spanish Empire expanded across the Atlantic to the Americas, more efficient long-distance ships came along rapidly, their development prodded by increasing demands. The transition from galleys to galleons was so swift that by the time the Spanish Armada set out for England, seventeen years after Lepanto, galleys accounted for roughly ten percent of the ships in the fleet, and most of them, due to their clumsiness and slowness, were kept in the reserve at the rear and out of the main battle lines.

Lepanto resulted in almost none of the changes that might have seemed likely in 1571—the Europeans did not reclaim much lost territory, let alone expand into the Ottoman Empire. No significant changes occurred in Arabic countries, or in Egypt. The military value of galleys continued their steady decline. European divisions did not lessen. But there were important changes nonetheless: the value of expansion into the Far East and the Americas became apparent, which cut out the Ottoman middlemen in a lot of Asian trade, and did a complete avoidance of it through America. The state of European politics remained chaotic for two centuries, and tricky after that. European assurance strengthened and grew. Perhaps the one European state that made the most of the Lepanto divide was Portugal, which maintained a good-sized navy, operated shipping ventures throughout the world, and got rich on the slave trade.

But even as the ships that fought the watershed battle slipped into memory, Lepanto took on a larger-than-life image in art. In Venice, the ninety-year-old artist Titian turned down a commission to paint a mural in the Doges' Palace on the subject of Lepanto, and so the task went to a young artist, Jacopo Robusti, who was known as Tintoretto; he proposed to do the work for no charge, and included an assurance to remove his work if another more preferable should be offered to the Doge in the next two years. This was a clever move, for the huge Lepanto painting in the Doges' Palace established Tintoretto's reputation and set him up for years. Titian sent two considerably smaller Lepanto allegorical paintings to Felipe II, who was as satisfied with them as he ever was with anything.

Lepanto also spawned vast quantities of verse—most of it didactic and tiresome—which served to keep the story of the battle alive, and to imbue it with a kind of theatrical gallantry that the genuine event singularly lacked. The heroic tale was much esteemed by Mary, Queen of Scots—who declared herself ready to marry Don Juan of Austria, if he had not been a bastard—and by her son, James VI of Scotland and I of England who in youth wrote his own long narrative in verse about the battle; when the work was eventually published, it was accompanied by an indignant apologia by a Protestant churchman attempting to excuse the king's puerile romance with Catholic causes. Other poetic outpourings were authored as part of various commemorative occasions, and tended to the kind of bombastic civic sentimentality that remained popular through the Victorian Era.

Starting almost immediately after Lepanto and continuing on for two centuries came a fashion for pulpits made in the form of ships' prows, for the most part out of regard for the Lepanto triumph—except in England, where such pulpits commemorated the sinking of the Spanish Armada. At the start of the craze it was limited to churches with direct associations with the action itself, but as time went by the style spread to places wishing to appear to have such an association, to look courtly, or to indicate there was someone buried on the church grounds who was reputed to have fought at Lepanto. Many of those claims appear to be less than accurate, for in at least three cases, if the dates of the self-proclaimed Lepanto veterans are correct, the men fought there while younger than eight—not impossible, but highly unlikely. Still, the look of European churches bears the memory of Lepanto to this day, and reveals how much that battle caught the public attention.

Due to the lack of participation in the Holy League, France was in a position to do more than simply help Sokolli deal with the Venetians. With so many soldiers assisting the Holy League, common interest took the upper hand: for one of the few times in Anglo-French relations, the English and the French entered into a trade agreement, one providing that English ships would bring their goods to French ports for European distribution, in exchange for which the French would give preferential trade rates to English merchants for salt, spices, and silks. This annoyed the Spanish, who had good reason to assume they could call the shipping-and-trade tune for most of western Europe now that the Ottomans were out of the mixture; only the belief that it would diminish Felipe's reputation as a Catholic ruler to deal with Protestant England stopped the Spanish from any real effort to undermine the trade agreement between England and France, but the arrangement continued to fester in Felipe's ruminations as relationships between England and Spain deteriorated.

With the death of Pope Pius V on May 1, 1572, the crusading fervor of the Holy League faltered, abetted in that hesitation by Felipe II, who had been dragging his heels about the Ottomans since his celebrations about Lepanto, claiming that Spanish territories in the New World needed more of his naval attention. They certainly produced more wealth than skirmishes with Ottoman galleys did, and spread Spanish influence throughout the world rather than limiting it to the eastern end of the Mediterranean Basin. Stating this new policy, he did not dispatch Spanish ships to the Holy League's summer campaign— which, without the Spanish, was more form than substance in any case—that had been intending to block critical Ottoman harbors to dry up their major trade centers, and to make a lightning strike to reclaim Cyprus. Don Juan waited for his half-brother's orders to embark, while Marcantonio Colonna took charge of the odds and ends of the fleet on short skirmishes which proved largely ineffective, but wonderful exercises in public relations, for the fewer engagements the Holy League fought, the greater the European sense of confidence became.

When the decision was made to summon another fleet to set out for North Africa and the Near East, Felipe—typically—hesitated. He thought it was unnecessary, and disrespect to the late Pope, who ought to be properly mourned for at least six months. When the King of Spain finally decided that Don Juan should set out for Palermo, he sent his half-brother on his way undersupplied and without sufficient funds to carry out his orders. After a prolonged council with Don Juan de Cardona and his fellow-officers, Don Juan informed his half-brother that, regretfully, he must return to Messina, since he would be unable to raise men enough to carry out the expedition Felipe had asked to have. Felipe responded by officially ordering Don Juan's return to Messina, where the spring and summer were spent with the Spanish galleys making occasional sallies into the Adriatic and the Aegean as a show of force but otherwise avoiding any risk of battle.

There were a few exceptions to this largely pro forma naval drive.

In one, the Marquis of Santa Cruz, coming upon the galley of the no-torious Hamet Bey patrolling with the Turkish fleet, managed to cut the Turk's ship out from the rest, and prepared to engage the Turk in battle. Hamet Bey made ready by sending most of his soldiers into the rigging to have a better line of fire for his archers and his arque-busiers, and clearing the decks in anticipation of boarding attempts, taking charge of the decks himself, and striding up and down them as the ships prepared to close. But Hamet Bey was deeply loathed by his galley slaves, and the pace oarsman managed to get hold of Hamet Bey as he passed along the oarsmen's outrigger to order his ship around toward Santa Cruz's. Using the only weapons he had—his teeth—the pace oarsman attacked Hamet Bey, then passed him— immobilized by the shock of his injury—to the oarsmen on the bench behind him. According to Santa Cruz's report, when he boarded the Turkish galley he found Hamet Bey's corpse on the deck, bleeding from over one hundred human bites, the archers and arquebusiers afraid to come down from the rigging for fear of receiving similar treatment.

Another odd encounter that summer—it could hardly be called a fight—took place near Crete where four Venetian war galleys, escort-ing a dozen round ships bringing supplies and trade goods to the is-land, came upon half a dozen galliots apparently on a slaving raid. The Ottoman ships slipped around the island only to be pursued by the galleys; they circled the island twice before they were forced to break off the unproductive pursuit and watched while the Ottoman galliots fled out to sea.

For the next year, the Spanish galleys remained virtually unused while Felipe worried about the problems he faced in the Netherlands, where a rebellion had taken form and was aimed at being rid of Span-ish control, dividing Felipe's attention and increasing his general paranoia. Many soldiers who might have been posted aboard Don Juan's galleys were instead ordered to the north, diminishing the fleet's effectiveness still further, and providing yet another excuse for the Spanish to withdraw support from the Holy League, claiming that Venice's treaty with the Ottoman Empire had betrayed the rest of Europe, and for which Spain would have to reconsider its commitment to the Holy League. During those long months of inactivity Don Juan seems to have taken Felipe's slights in stride, only occasionally asking his brother to find a use for him, and to support the Holy League in securing Mediterranean ports for European merchants, which could benefit Spain as well as other European countries.

Pope Pius V's successor, Gregory XIII—the Pope who amended the calendar to the one we use now—was furious when he found out about what he called Venice's duplicity, for he was aware that the foremost naval presence keeping the Ottomans in check was the Venetian, and that without their continued support, the Holy League would falter. He swore to withhold Vatican support for the European naval forces unless the Venetians could be made to abjure their treaty and once again unite with the Christian ships. Unlike the Pope, Venice knew most of the Ottoman naval apparent rearming was more cosmetic than threatening, and declined to set aside their bargain.

With Venice out of the picture, the Holy League was now almost totally dependent on Spain, which meant Felipe II, and he was disenchanted with the Holy League for a host of obvious and clandestine reasons. But disinclined though he was for Spain to engage in any direct sea battles with any Ottoman ships, there was the matter of Tunis, which the Spanish had regarded as part of their hegemony, and since Felipe feared that Tunis would slip away from Spanish influence now that Uchiali had become such a powerful man in the Ottoman court, plans were made to secure it completely for Spain. Tunis was one of the regions of northern Africa where corsairs preyed upon Spanish ships returning from the New World, and one that would provide Spain a base to keep the corsairs in check. To make it more symbolically attractive for Spain, it was Uchiali who had taken Tunis for the Ottomans a few years before, now giving Felipe an excellent excuse to flex a little seagoing muscle. Spain still controlled the fortress of La Goletta that stood at the entrance to the channel leading from the sea to the Bay of Tunis, making a convenient launch-point for a direct assault on Tunis.

Believing that the campaign would be a quick and easy one, Felipe sent orders to Don Juan of Austria, at the Holy League's anchorage in Sicily. Whether or not he actually wanted to use his half-brother for this task, Felipe knew that slighting the hero of Lepanto by refusing him further commissions could work to his disadvantage, so that little as he wished to add to Don Juan's splendid reputation, he realized it would be a grave mistake to keep the admirable young man out of the fight.

26

DON JUAN DE AUSTRIA

LTHOUGH HE WAS caught up in the ideals of chivalry from youth, Don Juan seems never to have confused those exalted sentiments with the reality of war, so he was understandably dismayed when he received an imperial command from Felipe in early September all but compelling the fleet to set out for Africa at the beginning of the storm season. On the second anniversary of Lepanto, October 7, 1573, the Holy League ships left Messina, bound for Tunis, across the Mediterranean, with slightly more than one hundred galleys. The fleet was supported by almost fifty supply ships and carried just under 20,000 infantry from Hapsburg countries and Italy, and they arrived at La Goletta the next afternoon.

Felipe II relied on the utter cooperation of Mulyeh Mahomet, the brother of the actual ruler at Tunis, who had withdrawn with his forces inland to the sacred city Kairouan, leaving Tunis in European hands with almost no hint of fighting, subject to the authority of a local ruler who was completely under Spanish influence. In terms of Spanish assessment, Tunis had the appearance of a success achieved even more easily than Lepanto.

Don Juan ordered repairs and improvements on the fortress of La Goletta and the city fortifications of Tunis itself—both much needed, and an essential part of the Spanish presence. The projects were worked on steadily, and with careful supervision, involving roughly thirty percent of the city's work force, and completed while the weather was still fairly good. Satisfied that he had done what was expected of him, Don Juan and most of the European ships left Tunis for Sicily on November 1, Don Juan bringing with him a lion cub, said to have been found in the ruins of Carthage, which he kept as a pet, giving the cub run of his cabin, and generally treating it like a puppy. It was the only spoil of war he ever took for himself.

Just because there was a peace of sorts between the Europeans and the Ottomans did not mean that both sides were not still employing spies to keep tabs on one another. Reports flew between Constantinople and the European capitals regularly, the spies doing their utmost to make themselves useful to their masters, which is why not all their reports were accurate. This accounts for the report waiting for Don Juan in Sicily upon his return—provided by Felipe II—that the Ottomans had spent the winter building an even bigger fleet than the one they lost at Lepanto, and they would shortly be setting out to engage the Holy League in battle.

Don Juan was well-regarded by the Turks: they admired his magnanimity and his sense of what today might seem good sportsmanship, such as sending children captured as part of harems back to Constantinople with no demand for ransom, and allowing Islamic galley slaves to worship Allah as their faith required. Don Juan had enough other information to doubt the report of a second, larger, better equipped fleet headed their way, but he was also fairly sure that the Sultan had ships enough to retake Tunis if Felipe should decide to leave it inadequately protected. Felipe, true to his nature, was beginning to second-think his hold on Tunis, and began to suppose that the Spanish conquest of the port city would only serve to prolong the Spanish war with the Ottoman naval forces. His hesitation proved costly for Spain, for in September of 1574, Tunis was retaken by its rightful ruler, and La Goletta fell immediately thereafter. Felipe had been warned of this possibility, but could not summon up his determination to issue the orders—and more importantly, set aside the finances—to ensure the Spanish hold on the African coast would continue.

For an excuse to offer the other members of the Holy League to account for this change of affairs, Felipe could indicate the rapidly developing situation in the New World that demanded a greater Spanish presence. There had been some uprisings among the natives—in large part due to the catastrophic introduction of measles into the population—who were horrified at seeing the death of so many of their people while the Europeans usually recovered from the "spots," as the disease was called. Felipe ordered more soldiers and more monks to take the matter in hand, and that detracted from the situation in Tunis. There had also been flare-ups in the Netherlands in the wake of the Duke of Alba's excesses among the Protestants; in response to this, Felipe had ordered Luis de Requesens—who had served Don Juan so ably at Lepanto—to the Netherlands to try to cobble together some kind of peace that did not entail any religious compromise on Spain's part, a goal the Pope was inclined to approve, and one he considered more urgent than Tunis or the neglect of Don Juan, which was increasingly marked.

The previous spring, just as Don Juan was preparing to make another attempt at getting the money to return to Tunis, fearing that it might be lost if not properly supplied and garrisoned, he was ordered by Felipe to make no attempt to reoccupy Tunis; apparently, aside from escalating New World preoccupations, Felipe believed the hints he had been given that Don Juan wanted a throne of his own—a suspicion that was inadvertently underscored by Pope Gregory's public support of Don Juan. In various of his official statements, the Pope declared that he believed Don Juan had earned a throne of his own for all he had done for Spain and the Church, and while he intended this throne to be in the New World, as an extension of present colonial policy and the security of the Spanish presence, that part of the

Pope's endorsement was overlooked, and Felipe's paranoia regarding his brother surged into new life, abetted by Antonio Perez, who had replaced Ruy Gómez da Silva, the chief Dove among Felipe's ministers. Perez worked constantly to discredit Don Juan at court—not very hard to do, given Felipe's state of mind—and through his activities to cut off any chance Don Juan might have for further military or political advancement. The viceroyalties of the various Spanish *Audiencias* were filled by others.

Don Juan, usually a very careful man, made a serious tactical mistake at that time when he agreed that he thought he was deserving of the right to use the title of Highness instead of Excellency just at the point that Felipe's trepidation about his half-brother was in full cry. Had he spoken at another time, he might have been able to make his point heard without creating more alarms in the ever mistrustful Felipe. It may be that he was given advice calculated to work against his interests, or it may be that, with the Pope endorsing his desire for promotion, Don Juan believed that he would have a strong position with the King of Spain. Whatever the reason for his timing, it backfired badly, and Perez made a point of reminding Felipe of Don Juan's perfidy as often as he could. With Don Juan far from court, Perez succeeded in discrediting Don Juan in his brother's eyes while he enhanced his own position as a protector of the crown.

But Perez's court days were numbered: he was carrying on an affair with Gómez da Silva's widow, the Princess of Eboli, who had been Felipe's mistress since her husband's death—and perhaps prior to his death. She passed on to Perez everything she learned from Felipe, information which Perez used to excellent advantage. Don Juan's secretary discovered that Perez was doing his utmost to discredit Don Juan, and kept track of the various exaggerations, fantasies, and lies that Perez was fostering in Felipe, as well as his private activities, which proved his undoing. Perez's duplicity was discovered in July, 1579, and his fall from royal favor was rapid and complete. But in spite of demonstrating that most of the supposed information that Perez had provided to Felipe was the product of deliberate malice, it did not restore Don Juan to believability with Felipe—convinced of Don Juan's malevolence and ambition, Felipe sought other sources to confirm it, and continued to refuse to support any project that his half-brother was part of. This included the enterprise of England, a proposal that had the full support of Pope Gregory.

This scheme was a plan to overthrow Elizabeth of England— propounded by exiled English Catholics—in favor of Mary, Queen of Scots, and then to seal the dynasty by marrying Don Juan to Mary, providing a return of Catholicism to England, and an ongoing political tie to Spain and Austria for the English royals, and through that association making it possible to form the greatest seagoing federation in history. Don Juan, somewhat more realistic about the situation than the Pope, pointed out that all this depended on Elizabeth's vastly capable network of spies learning nothing about the proposed rescue of Mary until it had been accomplished—unlikely at best—and then no one in the country rushing to defend the queen, another unlikely supposition. Convinced the plan would fail, Don Juan politely declined to participate in it, vexing English Catholics for his lack of faith in their devotion, but very likely sparing himself and England from fighting a religious civil war. He had been made aware that Mary was not averse to the match if Don Juan were legitimized, a qualification that further persuaded him to turn down the proposition, since he knew that was highly unlikely to happen, at least not while Felipe II was King of Spain.

Meanwhile in the Netherlands, William of Orange—a prince Felipe disliked almost as much as he disliked Don Juan—had assumed leadership of the Protestant rebels and was making real headway on their behalf. Felipe realized that he must have someone as popular as William to enforce the Spanish-Catholic position, and that capable as de Requesens was, he lacked the charisma that

Don Juan possessed. Burying his own misgivings—and they were many—Felipe ordered Don Juan to leave Sicily for the Netherlands to take over the governorship from his old comrade, Luis de Requesens, bring the rebels to heel, and restore the True Faith to the Netherlands.

27

VENETIAN DÉNOUEMENT

WITH THE OPPORTUNITY for prosperity once again present in the Venetian Empire, an optimism returned to the populace, and as the population soared, Venice once again strove to put itself in the forefront of the commercial world. This was not as readily done as was first supposed, for the wealth coming in from the New World and the Far East created limitations on the Venetian marketplace that it had not previously experienced. But the city was in a burst of civic renewal, and the public buildings, the churches, and the palaces of wealthy merchants were made more glorious with every passing month while La Serenissima was once again the tourist attraction it had been for more than six hundred years.

In July, 1574, the new, young King of France, Henri III, who had shortly before been King of Poland but was summoned back to France upon the death of his brother, Charles IX, made a visit to Venice en route home, for the stated purpose of keeping out of reach of the infuriated Poles, but with a few economic and diplomatic matters to discuss with the Doge and the Consiglii. To mark this occasion, Venice suspended all its sumptuary laws and settled in for a fine time filled with banquets, aquatic displays, processions, parades, musical entertainments, performances by singers, dancers, actors, and acrobats. The twenty-three-year-old Henri had assignations with the most famous courtesans in the city. And he was shown a war galley at the Arsenal, from the laying of a keel to launching, all done in a day. This set the stage for some serious discussions.

Doge Alvise Mocenigo I urged Henri to help Venice in dealing with the overbearing Felipe II of Spain, who, at least from the Venetian point of view, had been blundering about from misadventure to misadventure since the victory at Lepanto, and was in need of some reining in. The Doge pointed out the many Spanish slaughterings of Protestants in the Netherlands—he chose to ignore the Saint Bartholomew's Day Massacre in France two years earlier—and the need for men of goodwill to restore religious tolerance among the peoples of Europe. This put Henri in a difficult position, for he had ministers to answer to upon his arrival back home, so he was unwilling to commit himself to any firm policy. Upon his departure— another magnificent occasion—he promised he would remember Venice with thanks and admiration.

Aside from the heavy-handed policies of the Spanish, things were looking very good for the Venetians: the favorable relationship they had long enjoyed with France would be preserved, they had maintained their truce with the Ottomans, crops had been good all through eastern Europe and so shipping was up, and expanding once again to distant markets in Ottoman territory. Venetians were looking forward to riding the crest of Lepanto for some years ahead.

But by the autumn of 1576 the Black Plague had come to Venice, and it remained there until the following summer. The city lost fifteen percent of its population in those months—nowhere near as deadly as the epidemic of 1345, which claimed almost a third of the people of Europe, but still disastrous to the prosperity of the time. As the city emerged from the epidemic, Doge Mocenigo died and was succeeded by that veteran of Lepanto, Sebastian Venier, now eighty-one, and deeply conscious of the need to restore Venice and its fortunes as swiftly as possible, so as not to lose all the advantages Lepanto had gained them. His short reign was marked by a terrible fire that destroyed much of the Doges' Palace, and almost resulted in its being torn down. With his death three months after the fire, for many Venetians Lepanto entered the realm of the past instead of the recent present, and Venice devoted itself to other problems than the ones that had led to and devolved from Lepanto.

28

DON JUAN'S DÉNOUEMENT

A S ALWAYS, WHEN discussing Don Juan de Austria, the figure of Felipe II looms large, and never more so than in the events that led to the end of his short life. When assessing Felipe's seemingly irrational handling of his half-brother, it is wise to keep in mind that being born to the role of monarch of the wealthiest empire in the world (which Spain was at that time) is hardly a prescription for normality for anyone, and Felipe was not without problems that would have beset him had he been born in a goatherd's hovel in the meanest quarter of the country. Compulsive, rigid, often depressed, Felipe saw enemies all around him, men envious of his power and position, and never more than in his soft-spoken, charming, handsome, clever, courageous, illegitimate sibling.

As an ardent Catholic, Don Juan—usually more humane than most of those in his class at that period—shared Felipe's zeal for their faith, and found the Protestant inclination toward political as well as religious self-determinism a sign of dangerous immorality. He was an aristocrat at heart, one who considered liberty a depraved concept, likening it to a disease that would corrupt all men. He was typical of well-born men of his time, believing that most humans were in need of someone to lead them, to guide them, to think for them, and that without aristocrats to do that, there would be dire consequences for all of humanity. He regarded efforts toward secularism as potentially disastrous—which for his class, they were.

Like Felipe, Don Juan was horrified at the thought of heresy, and for him, any religion other than Roman Catholicism was unquestionably heresy, and as dangerous as Islam to the True Faith. Just as Felipe could not reconcile himself to granting religious rights to non-Catholics, so Don Juan believed it was his responsibility to return the Netherlands to the Church of Rome as mercifully as possible, and to eliminate Protestantism in Hapsburg territories, at least to the extent that he would require Catholicism of all citizens. Don Juan stopped short of endorsing the Duke of Alba's methods—systematic torture and slaughter on a large scale was repugnant to Don Juan. He did intend to reestablish Spanish government, but expressed within the context of the ancient traditions of the Netherlands. He was overjoyed to have an official position at last, and one he felt he could discharge well—his mother was from the Netherlands (in fact, she still lived there), and he spoke Flemish—since he was not inclined to allow any more outrages like those the Duke of Alba had permitted.

Ordered by Felipe to take the short route from Sicily to the Netherlands—through France—Don Juan found himself set about by restrictions: he could be accompanied by an escort of twelve and all must ride, he must keep his route a secret, he could carry no more than 20,000 ducats for his initial expenses as governor. Felipe also charged Don Juan with a somewhat more awkward mission: Don Juan was to convince his mother, whom he had not seen since he was a child, to abandon her very pubic, very expensive loose living in the Netherlands for quiet convent life in Spain, to spare the Hapsburgs further embarrassment from her outrageous conduct. Considering his upbringing with his foster parents in Spain, this commission must have caused the future governor a number of qualms, but he pledged to undertake to do it.

Don Juan took his own route into the Netherlands, avoiding the old Lorraine trade route. As if in anticipation of his meeting with his mother, he stopped off in Spain to see his foster mother, Magdalena de Ulloa, now a widow, and while there made his own preparations for his journey: he stained his face with walnut-juice and went into France disguised as his comrades' part-Moorish groom. As a soldier, he could take care of horses, and having been brought up in the countryside, he managed to fit into the lives of other servants as they traveled, passing through France virtually unnoticed—until they reached Paris, where Don Juan conspicuously fell in love with the talented, glamorous, licentious, clever Marguerite de Valois, sister to Henri III—the same fellow who had had such a good time in Venice.

Paris was a new experience for Don Juan. He had never been in so diverse a society as he found there, or so secular a one. Those Catholics who supported their faith also supported the disgraceful Saint Bartholomew's Day Massacre, a very shocking breach of proper conduct so far as Don Juan was concerned. He was doubly shocked to see the rhetoric of chivalry usurped by politicians and non-military nobility for their own purposes, many of them oppugant to the stated goals of the chivalric code. He found it difficult to reconcile his high regard for his beloved with Marguerite's hopes that after establishing himself as governor in the Netherlands, Don Juan might turn over the southern, French-speaking portion of the country to France, as a favor to her. These conflicting perceptions ate at him as he continued north to restore the Netherlands to a standard that he was beginning to think no one still believed in but himself.

Unfortunately, Don Juan had to arrive during the aftermath of Alba's army's havoc at Antwerp, an appalling debacle that saw unpaid soldiers turned loose indiscriminately on the people of that city to loot, kill, rape, and raid. Over 7,500 Antwerp residents were slaughtered, inflaming sentiments throughout northern Europe and bringing William of Orange, with his little army, to defend the Netherlands. William of Orange was called the Silent, meaning like a cat William the Sneaky, not the Unspeaking—and the adept way in which he used his small band of followers revealed just how richly he deserved his appellation. He did his best to maintain order in the country, and to preserve the people from religious persecution in any form whatsoever, all without provoking a direct confrontation with the Spanish, which he was almost certain to lose—a loss that could lead to the extermination of Protestantism in Hapsburg countries throughout Europe.

Don Juan's meeting with his mother in Luxembourg proved to be a dicey affair—Barbara wanted her now well-placed son to increase her annual allowance of 3,000 ducats, and he was expected to convince her to leave—she finally consented for her son's sake, but with a last word to him that was intended to sting: "I was wrong to call you the emperor's son," she told Don Juan, aware that if he had not heard of her dalliances during her affair with Charles V, he soon would. This farewell was soon known to every merchant, noble, priest, vagabond, soldier, housewife, and tavern-keeper in the Netherlands, and it did not make Don Juan's situation any easier. He did his best to make up for past failings, paying his soldiers as much as he could, and paying for supplies instead of pillaging them; gradually he made a little headway in gaining the good opinion of the Netherlanders, but the cost of it was high, and high in more than money.

Between his emotional turmoil over his mother and his infatuation with Marguerite de Valois, the resentment of the people toward Spanish religious excesses, the influence of William of Orange, and the demands of his position, success was beginning to tell on him. By the time his old friend and kinsman, Alessandro Farnese, arrived in the Netherlands with an army of 10,000 reinforcements, he saw that Don Juan was worn out, physically exhausted, and falling ill from stress.

Officially Don Juan attributed his poor condition to the chilly, inclement weather, but others suspected he might be the victim of poison. He was also wracked with self-doubt, for he began to see that his obedience to his half-brother had not redounded to his benefit, nor,

he was beginning to suspect, was it ever likely to do so. Now he spoke of taking monkish vows and withdrawing from the world as his father had. When he was almost stabbed by an agent of the English, he appeared to suffer a kind of breakdown, but instead of a monastery, he withdrew to Namur, publicly wishing to put himself in a place with superior security and fine communications. He would also be closer to Marguerite, who was bound for nearby Liège. Their meeting and subsequent idyll was the talk of the town for months, and for the time it lasted, he seemed very much his old self.

But this was to be the last happiness of his life. He soon showed symptoms of typhoid fever, and died in a dovecote at Namur on October 1, 1578. His heart was interred at Namur, his embalmed corpse was cut into pieces and carried in saddlebags to Madrid, where he was reassembled and laid to rest beside Charles V, a belated admission of familial recognition, coming too late in so many ways—not only posthumously, but after Don Juan had begun to doubt the connection himself.

29

AFTERTHOUGHTS

EPANTO IS PERHAPS the most contradictory battle of the sixteenth century: it was the epitome of galley warfare, and the last of it; it was an unexpected triumph for the Europeans over the Ottomans, but it changed very little for either side; it had the most innovations in ships' design brought into battle in the last four centuries, yet it used them traditionally, positioning arquebusiers like archers, and saving their main efforts for grappling, boarding, and hand-to-hand combat; it glorified chivalric and pious principles even as it employed them cynically for unchivalric ends; it drove the Ottomans from the seas, yet it made Ottoman land forces that much more formidable over the next eighty years.

Without it, the Spanish exploitation of the New World would have been considerably slowed; with it, the slave trade expanded to the Americas. Without it, Europe would have been commercially bankrupted by business losses in maritime trade; with it, Europe and the Ottomans spent themselves into maritime military nearbankruptcy. Without it, Europe's religious wars were likely to have become increasingly divisive; with it, the difference between tolerance and intolerance of religious differences became more exclusionarially drawn. For all it did for naval advances, Europeans made the most of them in commercial dealings, not military ones. In fact, it changed very little in the military-diplomatic sense, and it changed almost everything in the socio-cultural sense. It could have led to a climate of greater understanding between the Islamic Ottomans and the Christian Europeans, but neither side was willing to extend itself beyond the practical commercial treaties that marked Ottoman-European relations for as long as the Ottoman Empire endured; echoes of that failure remain with us today.

Perhaps, had Lepanto been a land battle, it might not have become legend as rapidly or as totally as it did. Had it been fought on land, there would have been lasting evidence of its significance. Memorials might have been built on the spot, and the names of those thousands who fought it enrolled in stone. But as it is, Lepanto slipped away beneath the waves and into the imagination of those who were not there, making it perfect fuel for myth. Yet myth does not rob it of its importance, or lessen the impact it had on those who fought it. Whatever else it was or was not, this may describe it best: *La mayor jornada que vieron los siglos*—the greatest day's work we have seen done in centuries—Miguel Cervantes wrote, and it is hard to argue with him: he was there.

INDEX

Africa
  Coptic Christians in Egypt and
    Ethiopia, 21
  corsair attacks from ports in, 52
  Egypt, Ottoman control of, 35
  ports in, Ottoman control of, 51, 59
  slave trade, 56
  Tunis, Spanish control of, 178–79,
    181–83
Alba, Duke of, 183, 192, 193
Alessandrino, Cardinal, 75
Ali Ahmed, 70
Ali Pasha
  ambition, 116, 117–18
  background and popularity, 81
  Crete, failure to capture, 116
  in Famagusta campaign, 93
  kidnapping of oarsmen, 116
  at Lepanto
    battle lines, 128, 129, 132
    in command of Ottoman forces,
      117
    at damage to flagship, *Sultana*, 132
    death, 133
    strategy, 121
    Sultan's orders to, 122–23
    threatening of galley slaves, 121–22
  Nicosia, capture of, 78–79
Alvaro de Bazan, Don, 105, 135
Ambrosio, 126
Andrade, Gil d', 119, 121
arquebuses, 107–8
arrows and bows, 38, 107
Asturias, Don Carlos de, 65–66
Austria, Don Juan de. *See* Juan de
  Austria, Don
Austrian Hapsburgs, 50–51, 85
  See also Hapsburg Empire

Baglione, Astor, 87
Barbarigo, Agostino, 105, 121, 126, 134

basilisks, 94
Bayezid, 69
Bazan, Don Alvaro de, 105, 135
Bey, Hamet, 177
Black Plague, 188
Blomberg, Barbara, 63, 192, 194
boarding nets, 108
Bohemian paper-making industry,
  56–57
Borgia, Francisco, 105
bows and arrows, 38, 107
Bragadin, Antonio, 126
Bragadin, Marcantonio, 61, 87, 95,
  97–99
Brahe, Tycho, 58
Brenton *(bertoni)* ships, 161
Brothers of Saint Spiridion, 157–58
Byzantine Empire, 21, 30, 31–32

cannon, 37–38, 107–8
Capitana (ship), 138, 141
Carafa, Gian Pietro, 66
Cardona, Don Juan de, 105, 125, 129,
  139–40
Carlos de Asturias, Don, 65–66
Carlos I of Spain (Holy Roman
  Emperor Charles V), 50, 51,
  62–63, 64, 65
Catholic Church
  Inquisitorial Process, 25, 61–62, 66,
    67
  political competition within, Jesuit
    rise to power, 63
  Protestantism, response to, 24, 71
  Spanish influence over, 24, 52–53
  See also Papal States
Cervantes, Miguel, 159, 198
Charles IX, King of France, 60, 83, 187
Charles V, Holy Roman Emperor
  (Charles I of Spain), 62–63, 64,
  65

China, technological innovations in, 57

Christendom. *See* Europe; Holy League; Papal States

Clement VII, Pope, 52

Colonna, Marcantonio
background, 76
as Don Juan's senior commander, 105
Holy League commander, appointment as, 76, 79
in Lepanto battle, 76, 109, 121, 127–28
loot distribution guidelines, 153
negotiations between Genoese and Venetians, 76, 77–78
public relations exercises, 176
Rome, escort of Turkish prisoners to, 164

Colonna, Prospero, 159

Consiglios, 43

Constantinople
as center of Ottoman Empire, 19, 21, 33
Christians in, 21, 168, 170
shipbuilding in, 169, 170
See also Ottoman Empire

Coptic Christians, 21, 22

Corfu, 109, 112, 119, 155–56

Corinth Channel. *See* Lepanto battle

corsairs
extent of piracy, 26
fleets, escalation in size of, 48
Kara Hodja, 68, 111, 115–16, 151
Lepanto strategy, 121
preferred prey, 160–61
ship modifications, 38
Spanish ships, attacks on, 52, 178
strategies and tactics, 35–37
Sultan, relationship with, 34
Uchiali
appointment as admiral of fleet, 169
background, rise in power and ambition, 68, 69–70
in Crete campaign, 116
at Lepanto, 121, 129, 135, 137–38, 139, 140

navy, inability to rebuild, 167–68
Tunis, capture of, 178–79
Venetian ships, attacks on, 35, 47
Venice, attacks on, 111

Crete, 76–77, 116

Crimean Tartars, 57

Crusades, 31, 40–41

Cyprus
Famagusta
casualties, 95
galvanization of European anger, 60–61, 89, 91, 112
Ottoman advance to, 82, 87–88, 93–95
resupply of, 89–90
supply problems, 94
surrender and truce terms, 95, 97–98
truce violation, 60–61, 81–82, 98–99, 100–101
Nicosia, fall of, 78–79, 81–82
Ottoman landing on, 72–73
in Venetian empire, 41

Dandolo, Nicolo, 73, 81–82

d'Andrade, Gil, 119, 121

de, names including. *See part of name preceding preposition (e.g. Juan de Austria, Don)*

dei Medici, Cosimo, 83

della Roverei family, 76

Doges
marriage of Adriatic Sea, 34
Mocenigo, Alvise, 44, 45, 188
in Venetian governmental structure, 43
Venier, Sebastian, 188–89

Don, names beginning with. *See part of name following Don (e.g. Juan de Austria, Don)*

Doria, Giannandrea
ambition, 79
as Don Juan's senior commander, 105–6
hesitancy, 77–78, 111–12
Holy League commander, appointment as, 76
Lepanto strategy, 120–21, 126, 128

looting, eagerness for, 146
Pope's disapproval of, 155
technological recommendations,
    107–8
Uchiali, confrontation with, at
    Lepanto, 135, 145
Dragut, 70

Eboli, Princess of, 184
Elizabeth, Queen of England, 185
el Louck Ali. See Uchiali
England, 57, 175, 185
Europe
    captives, ransom of, 157
    Constantinople, enthusiasm for
        conquest of, 161–62
    Crusades, 31, 40–41
    engineering and technological
        advances, 20, 137
    ethnic diversity in, 15
    Famagusta seizure, galvanization of
        anger following, 60–61, 89, 91,
        112
    Genoese and Venetian rivalry, 45, 52,
        71–72, 76, 77
    Hapsburg disunity, 53
    Holy League, increased support for,
        88–89
    Lepanto battle, motives for, 20
    Lepanto officers, perceptions of, 155
    Lepanto triumph, outcomes of,
        173–74
    mercantile economy, wealth from
        New World, 23–24
    Ottoman aggression toward,
        following Lepanto battle,
        171–72
    Ottoman Empire, increase in
        hostilities toward, 31, 70, 72
    Ottoman expansion, fear of, 21, 59
    Philippine colonization, 57
    political problems, 24
    Protestantism, polarization of
        Christianity, 24, 71
    Reformation, 25, 163, 170
    vision of place in world, age of
        exploration, 163–64, 176

See also Holy League; Papal States;
    specific countries

Fabiani family, 76
Famagusta
    casualties, 95
    galvanization of European anger,
        60–61, 89, 91, 112
    Ottoman advance to, 82, 87–88,
        93–95
    resupply of, 89–90
    supply problems, 94
    surrender and truce terms, 95, 97–98
    truce violation, 60–61, 81–82,
        98–99, 100–101
Farnese, Alessandro, 65, 127, 135, 193
Felipe II
    Don Juan
        appointment as Netherlands
            governor, 186, 192
        dispatch of, to Palermo, 176
        jealousy and treatment of, 66,
            105–6, 165–66, 183–85, 191
        limitations on Holy League
            command, 105
    England, deterioration of relations
        with, 175
    in Hapsburg family line, 50
    Netherlands, problems in, 51, 177,
        183, 186, 192
    New World, preoccupation with, 176,
        183
    obsessive personality, religious
        fanaticism, 25, 61–62
    Tunis, plans to secure, 178–79,
        182–83
    Venice, disinclination to defend, 75
female arquebusier at Lepanto, Maria
    the Dancer, 146, 159
Ferdinand V of Castile and Leon, 50
flaming arrows, 38
France
    Charles IX, 60, 83, 187
    England, trade agreement with, 175
    Genoa, influence in, 42
    Hapsburg claims on, 60, 83
    Henri III, 187–88

France (*continued*)
Lepanto volunteers, 127
Ottoman intention to conquer, 170
Ottoman-Venetian peace
negotiations, assistance in, 99,
143–44
Frederick V of Germany, 49

galleasses, design and modification of,
106–8
galleons, design of, 173
Garcia de Toledo, Don, 106, 155, 161,
162
Genoa
French influence over, 42
Holy League membership, 60, 76, 77,
104, 107
Lepanto triumph, subdued
celebration of, 164–65
as Ottoman target, 32–33
Spanish influence and control over,
21, 45–46, 52, 75
Venice, rivalry with, 45, 52, 71–72, 76,
77
German States, 24, 49, 52
Ghazi, Osman al-, 32
Ghislieri, Antonio. *See* Pius V, Pope
Ghislieri, Paolo, 157
Giustiniani, Pietro, 138
Gómez da Silva, Ruy, 184
Granvelle, Cardinal, 75
Great Christ Risen Again (ship), 140
Greek fire, 37–38
Greeks. *See* Byzantine Empire
Gregory XIII, Pope, 178, 183–84, 185
Gulf of Lepanto. *See* Lepanto battle
Gulf of Patmas. *See* Lepanto battle
Guzman (ship), 140, 141

Hapsburg Empire
Austrian Hapsburg territories, 60
extent of, 49–50
France, claims on, 60, 83
Holy League involvement, 52, 59,
85
influence of, 61
internal problems, 50–53

Netherlands and, 50–51
Ottoman Empire, resistance to, 24,
49
split into Spanish and Hapsburg-
Lorraine (Austrian) lines, 50
Venice, disinclination to assist, 52
See also Spain
Hassan, 121
Henri III, King of France, 187–88
heretics. *See* Protestants and
Protestantism
Hieronymite Order, 63
Hodja, Kara (Karakoch), 68, 111,
115–16, 151
Hogg, Thomas (Hodge), 14, 139
Holland. *See* Netherlands
Holy League
chaplains, 104
commanders, 76, 79, 85, 105–6
constituents, 21, 59–60
Crete, planned attack at, 76–78
European support for, 88–89
fleet and armaments, 77, 106–8, 115,
127
food provisions, 80
formation of, 59–60, 71–72
public relations summer campaign,
176
Rhodes, planned attack at, 78–79
rivalries and internal conflicts, 71–72,
76, 77, 103–5, 113
Spain, dependence upon, 178
Tunis expedition, 181
uniforms, 104
volunteer soldiers, 21, 60, 127
waning interest in, 175–76
See also Lepanto battle
Holy Roman Emperor Charles V
(Charles I of Spain), 62–63, 64,
65
Holy Roman Emperor Frederick III
(Frederick V of Germany),
49
Hulegu, 32

Iroquois confederation, 56
Isabella the Catholic, 51, 62

Islamic culture and traditions
  in Baghdad, 32
  Mecca prayer flag, 129, 154
  offenses against, 98, 100
  in Ottoman Empire, 15, 21–23, 31, 138
  secular Turkish society, 172
  treatment of non-Islamic groups,
    21–23
  Turkish embrace and spread of,
    30–31, 33
Ivan, Czar "The Terrible" or "Awe-
  Inspiring," 55

James VI of Scotland and I of England,
  174
Japan, Western trade with, 56
Jenghiz Khan, 32
Jesuits, 63
Jews, 21–22, 62
Juana la Loca (Crazy Joan), 62
Juan de Austria, Don
  background, 63–65, 66
  Catholic faith and convictions, 191
  Corfu, discovery of supply ships at,
    155
  diplomacy and humility, 154
  Felipe II's jealousy and treatment of,
    66, 105–6, 165–66, 183–85, 191
  France, visit to, 193
  illness and death, 194–95
  at Lepanto
    in command of Holy League
      forces, 63, 85, 105
    credit for triumph, 163
    on flagship, Real, 131, 132
    generosity toward wounded
      soldiers, 153–54
    injury, 133, 154
    intelligence-gathering, 119–20
    restrictions on leadership, 105–6
    soldiers, encouragement of, 129
    strategy and battle lines, 113–14,
      120–21, 125, 126–28
    tour of ships following battle,
      145–46
    Venier, difficulties with, 112–13
    weaponry modification, 108

magnanimity, 153–54, 182
Marguerite de Valois, infatuation
    with, 193, 194
  mother, 63, 192, 194
  naval warfare, study of, 106
  Netherlands governorship, 186,
    192–93, 194
  Palermo mission, 176
  Spanish disapproval of, 163
  Tunis mission, 179, 181–82
  Turks, high regard by, 182
Juan de Cardona, Don, 105, 125, 129,
    139–40
Juan de Zuniga, Don, 75

Kara Hodja (Karakoch), 68, 111, 115–16,
    151
Knights of Malta, 83, 138, 141, 167
Knights of Saint John, 51, 107

La Serenissima. See Venice
Legazpe, Miguel Lopez de, 57
Lepanto battle
  Ali Pasha
    battle lines, 128, 129, 132
    in command of Ottoman forces,
      117
    at damage to flagship, Sultana, 132
    death, 133
    strategy, 121
    Sultan's orders to, 122–23
    threatening of galley slaves, 121–22
  artillery and technological
    innovations, 106–8, 132, 137
  casualties, 138, 139–40, 147, 149–50
  Christian galley slaves, 134, 147, 149
  contradictions of, 197–98
  destruction of ships, deliberate, 140
  Don Juan de Austria
    in command of Holy League
      forces, 63, 85, 105
    credit for triumph, 163
    on flagship, Real, 131, 132
    generosity toward wounded
      soldiers, 153–54
    injury, 133, 154
    restrictions on leadership, 105–6

Lepanto battle (*continued*)
  soldiers, encouragement of, 129
  strategy and battle lines, 113–14,
    120–21, 125, 126–28
  tour of ships following battle,
    145–46
  Venier, difficulties with, 112–13
  weaponry modification, 108
  end of, 141, 152–53
  as end of Ottoman expansion, 19
  female arquebusier, Maria the
    Dancer, 146, 159
  flagships, involvement of, 131,
    132–33
  fleet sizes, 106–7, 128
  force strengths, 149–50
  galley fleets, final use of, 173
  hardships and illnesses, 119–20,
    151–52
  historical accounts of, 14, 15
  intelligence-gathering, 115–16,
    119–20, 122, 125
  loot collection and distribution, 146,
    147, 150–52, 153
  Ottomans, difficult strategic position
    of, 137, 138
  Ottoman surrender and
    abandonment of ships, 145
  reasons for, 19, 27–28, 109
  Spanish financing of, 24
  start of, 106, 108–9, 128–32
  strategies, 111, 116–17, 120–21,
    122–23
  Uchiali in, 121, 129, 135, 137–38, 139,
    140
  volunteer soldiers, 21, 60, 127
Lepanto battle aftermath
  art and poetic commemorations,
    174–75
  changes engendered, 173–74
  disarray of Ottoman marine military,
    167
  honors and celebrations, 156,
    163–65
  outcomes for veterans, 157–59
Little Gallipoli. *See* Lepanto battle
Lopez de Legazpe, Miguel, 57

Loredan, Pietro, 44
Luis de Requesens, 105, 129, 183, 185

Maestrobiaggio, Giorgio (Gregorio),
    159
Magdalena de Ulloa, 64, 192–93
Maggior Consiglio, 43
Mahomet, Mulyeh, 181
Malta, Knights of, 83, 138, 141, 167
Malta, Siege of, 51
Mameluke Empire, 35
Margaret of Parma, 62–63, 65, 194
Marguerite de Valois, 193
Maria the Dancer, 146, 159
Martinengo, Nestor, 88
Mary, Queen of Scots, 174, 185
Massi, Francisco and Ana, 63–64
Maximillian I, 49
Medici, Cosimo dei, 83
Minor Consiglio, 43
Mocenigo, Alvise, 44, 45, 188
Mongol invasions, 31–32
Moors, 26, 51, 62
Morisco Revolt, 51, 70, 105
Most Serene Republic. *See* Venice
Mustapha, Lala
  Cyprus campaign, 60–61, 72, 78, 83
  Famagusta siege, 82, 94, 95
  Famagusta surrender truce, 95,
    97–99
  mixed support for, 81
  reputation of, 99–100
  as spy for Sultan, 68

Netherlands
  clock-making, 58
  Don Juan's governorship, 186, 192,
    193
  Duke of Alba's oppression of
    Protestants, 183, 192, 193
  Luis de Requesens's governorship,
    183, 185
  rebellion against Spanish rule, 51, 177,
    183
  Spanish control of, 50–51
  William of Orange's leadership of
    Protestants, 185, 193–94

New World
  European wealth from, 23–24
  Felipe II's preoccupation with, 176,
    183
  Spanish expansion to, 24, 45–46, 56,
    173, 176

Ochiali. *See* Uchiali
Ojeda, Captain, 141
Orsini family, 76
Ottoman Empire
  Constantinople
    as center of Ottoman Empire, 19,
      21, 33
    Christians in, 21, 168, 170
    shipbuilding in, 169, 170
  corsairs
    escalation in fleet size, 48
    extent of piracy, 26
    Lepanto strategy, 121
    modifications to ships, 38
    preferred prey, 160–61
    Spanish ships, attacks on, 52
    strategies and tactics, 35–37
    Sultan, relationship with, 34
    Venetian ships, attacks on, 35, 47
    Venice, attacks on, 111
  Crete, failure to conquer, 116
  Cyprus campaign, 72–73, 78–79,
    81–82
  ethnic and religious groups
    encompassed, 21–23
  Europe, aggression toward, following
    Lepanto battle, 171–72
  Europe, increase in hostilities toward,
    31, 70, 72
  European culture, misunderstanding
    of, 15, 100, 170
  expansion and conquests, 19, 20, 31,
    32, 35, 112
  Famagusta siege, 82, 87–90, 93–95,
    97–99
  inflation and devaluation of currency,
    170–71
  internal politics, 26
  Islamic religion and culture, 15,
    21–23, 31, 138
  labor-based economy, 23, 171
  Malta siege, 51
  Mediterranean, control of, 19, 31, 35
  navy
    development of, 32–33, 35, 48
    disarray of, 167
    disinclination to use, 169–70
    leaders, 26, 68–69, 169
    second navy, rumors of, 144, 149,
      153, 182
    shipbuilding problems, 169
  piracy, 20, 26, 32–33, 59
  Rhodes, base on, 72, 78, 79
  Sultan Selim II
    background and personality,
      67–68
    on execution of Christians in
      Constantinople, 168
    Famagusta capture, demand for, 93
    Lepanto battlement,
      reinforcement of, 101
    Lepanto strategy, 116–17, 122–23
    overland attacks on Europeans,
      plans for, 170
    Piale Pasha's command, relief of,
      82–83
    second navy, belief in existence of,
      144, 149
    Sokolli, reliance upon, 69
    Tunis, capture of, 178–79
  Venice, peace treaty with (1573), 83,
    84, 99, 143–44, 171
  Venice, trading rights treaty with
    (1479), 33–34, 111
  Venice and Venetian holdings,
    intention to conquer, 32–34,
    44–45, 72, 111, 112
  See also Lepanto battle

Papal States
  Catholic Church
    Inquisitorial Process, 25, 61–62,
      66, 67
    political competition within, Jesuit
      rise to power, 63
    Protestantism, response to, 24, 71
    Spanish influence over, 24, 52–53

Papal States (*continued*)
  celebration of Lepanto triumph, 164
  Clement VII, 52
  fear of Turkish vengeance, 165
  Gregory XIII, 183–84, 185
  Holy League membership, 60, 107
  Pius V
    austerity, 66–67
    background, rise to papacy, 66
    death, 175
    Don Juan, choice of, to command
      Holy League, 85
    Don Juan, crediting of, for
      Lepanto triumph, 163
    Doria's hesitancy at Lepanto,
      disapproval of, 155
    heretics, policies concerning, 67
    Holy League, formation of, 59, 60,
      71, 83, 104
    on Lepanto triumph, 143
    ransom of captured nephew, 157
    vision of triumph against
      Ottomans, 143
  Venice, relationship with, 42
Parma, Margaret of, 62–63, 65, 194
Pasha, Ali
  ambition, 116, 117–18
  background and popularity, 81
  Crete, failure to capture, 116
  in Famagusta campaign, 93
  kidnapping of oarsmen, 116
  at Lepanto
    battle lines, 128, 129, 132
    in command of Ottoman forces,
      117
    at damage to flagship, *Sultana,* 132
    death, 133
    strategy, 121
    Sultan's orders to, 122–23
    threatening of galley slaves, 121–22
  Nicosia, capture of, 78–79
Paul IV, Pope, 66
Perez, Antonio, 184
Philip II of Spain. *See* Felipe II
Philippine colonization, 57
Piale Pasha, 72, 77, 82–83
pirates. *See* corsairs

Pius V, Pope
  austerity, 66–67
  background, rise to papacy, 66
  death, 175
  Don Juan, choice of, to command
    Holy League, 85
  Don Juan, crediting of, for Lepanto
    triumph, 163
  Doria's hesitancy at Lepanto,
    disapproval of, 155
  heretics, policies concerning, 67
  Holy League, formation of, 59, 60, 71,
    83, 104
  on Lepanto triumph, 143
  ransom of captured nephew, 157
  vision of triumph against Ottomans,
    143
popes. *See* Papal States
Portugal, 57–58, 174
Protestants and Protestantism, 24, 61,
  67, 71, 185, 194

Quirini, Marcantonio, 82, 90, 116, 126,
  133
Quixada, Luis, 64

Real (ship), 109, 127, 132, 146
Reformation, 25, 163, 170
  See also Protestants and Protestantism
Republic of Genoa. *See* Genoa
Requesens, Luis de, 105, 129, 183, 185
Rhodes, 72, 78–79
Robusti, Jacopo (Tintoretto), 174
Rome. *See* Papal States
Russia, 55, 57

Saint John, Knights of, 51, 107
Saint Spiridion, Brothers of, 157–58
San Giovanni (ship), 140
Santa Cruz, Marquis of, 121, 128, 138,
  140, 177
Savoy, galleys from, 107, 140
Scotto, Onorio, 90
Selim II "The Grim"
  background and personality, 67–68
  on execution of Christians in
    Constantinople, 168

Famagusta capture, demand for, 93
Lepanto battlement, reinforcement
    of, 101
Lepanto strategy, 116–17, 122–23
overland attacks on Europeans, plans
    for, 170
Piale Pasha's command, relief of,
    82–83
second navy, belief in existence of,
    144, 149
Sokolli, reliance upon, 69
Shakespeare, William, 57
shipbuilding technology and innovation
    galleasses, 106–8
    galleons, 173
    merchant ships, 20
    standardization of design, 46–47
    Venetian war galleys, 37, 46
Sicilian galleys, 76, 77
Silva, Ruy Gómez da, 184
Sirocco, Mahomet, 68, 93, 122, 133,
    134
Society of Jesus, 63
Sokolli, Mahomet
    Christians in Constantinople,
        treatment of, 168, 170
    Cyprus, command of fleet landing on,
        72
    position and personal qualities, 69
    Uchiali, rivalry with, 169
    Venice, peace negotiations with, 83,
        84, 99, 143–44, 171
South America, exploration of, 57–58
Spain
    Catholic Church, influence over, 24,
        52–53
    England, deterioration of relations
        with, 175
    exploration and colonialism, 25, 52,
        57–58
    Felipe II
        Don Juan, jealousy and treatment
            of, 66, 105–6, 165–66, 183–85,
            191
        in Hapsburg family line, 50
        Netherlands, problems in, 51, 177,
            183, 186, 192

New World, preoccupation with,
    176, 183
obsessive personality, religious
    fanaticism, 25, 61–62
Tunis, plans to secure, 178–79,
    182–83
Venice, disinclination to defend,
    75
Genoa, influence and control over, 21,
    45–46, 52, 75
under Hapsburg control, 50
Holy League membership, 59, 75,
    84–85, 107, 111, 178
Inquisition, 22, 51, 61–62
Lepanto strategy, 120
Netherlands, control of, 51, 177,
    183
New World, expansion to, 24, 45–46,
    56, 173, 176
religious rigidity, 25–26, 51, 53, 67
ship design, 103
Tunis, presence in, 178–79,
    181–83
Stukeley, Thomas, 127, 157
Sultan. See Selim II "The Grim"
Sultana (ship), 129, 132, 151
Suluk, Mehmed, 68
Surian, Michele, 75

Tahmasp, Shah of Persia, 69
Tartars, 57
Tintoretto (Jacopo Robusti), 174
Titian, 174
Toledo, Don Garcia de, 106, 155, 161,
    162
Tunis, 178–79, 181–83
Turks
    conquest of Constantinople, 33
    conversion to Islam, 30–31
    economic connections, control of
        trade routes, 31
    expansionism, 32
    migration westward, 29–30
    Western and Celestial Turkish
        groups, 29
    See also Ottoman Empire
Tuscany, galleys from, 107, 126

Uchiali (el Louck Ali; Ochiali, Uchali)
    appointment as admiral of fleet, 169
    background, rise in power and
        ambition, 68, 69–70
    in Crete campaign, 116
    at Lepanto, 121, 129, 135, 137–38, 139,
        140
    navy, inability to rebuild, 167–68
    Tunis, capture of, 178–79
Ulloa, Magdalena de, 64, 192–93

Valois, Marguerite de, 193
Vandals, 39
van der Gheest, Johanna, 62
Venice
    Arsenal, 46–47, 111
    Black Plague, 188
    Byzantine influence in, 42–43
    Cyprus
        fall of Nicosia, 78–79, 81–82
        Ottoman landing on, 72–73
        in Venetian empire, 41
    decline of empire, 35
    Doge, Alvise Mocenigo, 44, 45, 188
    Famagusta
        casualties, 95
        galvanization of European anger
            toward Ottomans, 60–61, 89,
            91, 112
        Ottoman advance to, 82, 87–88,
            93–95
        resupply of, 89–90
        supply problems, 94
        surrender, truce terms, 95, 97–98
        truce violation by Ottomans,
            60–61, 81–82, 98–99, 100–101
    Genoa, rivalry with, 45, 52, 71–72, 76,
        77
    governmental structure, 43
    Henri III, King of France's visit to,
        187–88

Holy League membership, 60, 75,
    76–77, 100, 106–7, 126
on Lepanto triumph, 159–60, 174
mercantile economy, 39–42
military engagement, avoidance of,
    43, 47–48
Ottoman expansion, threat of,
    44–45
as Ottoman target, 32–33, 52, 111
prosperity and civic renewal,
    187–88
shipbuilding innovation, 35, 37,
    46–47, 103, 106–7
Sokolli, peace negotiations with, 83,
    84, 99, 143–44, 171
Sokolli, trust in, 69
treaty on separate peace with
    Ottomans (1573), 171
treaty on trading rights in Ottoman
    territory (1479), 33–34, 111
Venier, Sebastian
    Don Juan, alienation of, 112–13
    as Don Juan's senior commander,
        105–6
    election as Doge, death, 188–89
    Famagusta siege, response to, 90–91
    at Lepanto, 109, 133
Vienna, 172

weapons
    arquebuses, 107–8
    basilisks, 94
    cannon, 37–38, 107–8
    flaming arrows, bows, 38, 107
    Greek fire, 37–38
William of Orange "The Silent," 185,
    193–94

Zanne, Hieronimo, 76, 77
Zoroastrians, 22–23
Zuniga, Don Juan de, 75